New Food Shop Graphics

New Food Shop Graphics

Copyright © 2009 PIE BOOKS
All rights reserved. No part of this publication may be reproduced in any
form or by any means, graphic, electronic or mechanical, including
photocopying and recording by an information storage and retrieval
system, without permission in writing from the publisher.

PIE BOOKS
2-32-4, Minami-Otsuka, Toshima-ku, Tokyo 170-0005 JAPAN
Tel : +81-3-5395-4811   Fax : +81-3-5395-4812

e-mail : editor@piebooks.com   sales@piebooks.com
http://www.piebooks.com

ISBN978-4-89444-771-4 C3070
Printed in Japan

Cafes / Sweeteries カフェ／スウィーツ

10

はじめに

　飲食店のデザインには、私たちが生活するのに必要な「衣食住」すべての事柄が関わってきます。食はもちろんのこと、くつろいで過ごせる空間の創造や、コンセプトに合わせたスタッフの装い。同業他店と競合する上で、次の来店につなげるためには、サービス内容だけでなく、センスや雰囲気のいいお店であることも重要な要素です。思わず持ち帰りたくなるショップカード、ちょっとしたステイタスを感じるギフトボックス、素材のよさを伝えるビジュアル……。ロゴや内装、グラフィックツールなど、ショップアイデンティティを訴求するためのビジュアル開発は、店舗の条件に合わせてさまざまな形で展開されます。コンセプトを明確にビジュアル化することに、独自性と成功を生み出す要因があると言えるでしょう。

　本書は、飲食店のトータルデザイン作品集として、さまざまな業態の店舗の中で、デザイン性が高く、魅力的なショップを国内だけでなく海外からも幅広くピックアップし、約100店掲載しています。コンテンツは以下の3つに大別し、近年オープンしたお店を中心に紹介しています。

カフェ／スウィーツ　Cafes / Sweeteries
デリ／軽食　Delis / Light fare
レストラン／バー　Restaurants / Bars

　本書には、メニューブックやショップカード、コースターなど、実際にお店に足を運ばないと見られないものを多数収録しています。グラフィックツールに加え、各ショップの外装・内装も併せて掲載し、ショップデザインをトータルで紹介しています。グラフィックツールと、お店の雰囲気がどのように連動しているかをうかがい知ることができます。

　グラフィックデザイナー・インテリアデザイナー・ショップ企画経営に携わる方・プレス担当の方・プランナーなど、飲食店におけるデザイン戦略の資料として、さまざまなクリエイターや業界の皆様に活用いただける1冊となりましたら幸いです。

　最後になりましたが、お忙しいなかご協力くださり、快く作品をご提供くださいました方々に、この場を借りてお礼を申し上げます。

Foreword

Designing food and beverage establishments involves not only food, but "clothing and shelter" as well; in other words all three of what we call the necessities of life.
It goes without saying that key to the success of restaurants, bars, and other dining and drinking places are creating a relaxing ambience, plus styling staff and interiors to complement the chosen concept.
When it comes to competing with others in the same industry, scoring repeat business is not just a matter of service: tempting customers with tasteful surroundings and a welcoming atmosphere are equally important.
Shop cards customers will find themselves wanting to take home, gift boxes that endow just a hint of special status, visuals that reassure, and proclaim the high quality of the ingredients used...
Visuals that create and assert identity — logos, interiors, graphics and more — are developed to suit the conditions of each business.
One could say there are certain factors sure to encourage originality and success, by turning concepts into visuals in the clearest possible way.

New Food Shop Graphics offers a comprehensive overview of food and beverage establishment design, via a varied selection of around 100 standout examples from Japan and abroad chosen for their superlative design sense. The contents are divided broadly into the following three sections, with a focus on places that have opened in recent years.

Cafes / Sweeteries
Delis / Light fare
Restaurants / Bars

The book contains many examples of design — menu books, shop cards, coasters etc. — not usually accessible without actually visiting the premises. Including exteriors and interiors in addition to graphic tools provides a total introduction to shop design, and shows how graphic tools as visual elements are linked to the ambience of each establishment.

We hope this volume will serve as an invaluable design strategy reference for graphic designers, interior designers, those involved in shop planning and management, those charged with press and publicity matters, planners and others in the creative and hospitality industries.

Thank you to all those who so generously assisted in the production of New Food Shop Graphics by supplying examples of their work.

Editorial Notes

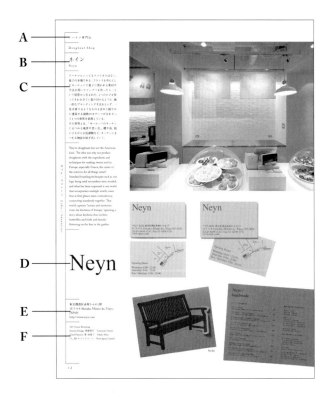

✤ クレジット・フォーマット　Credit Format

A ... 店舗種類　Type of business
B ... 店舗名称　Shop Name
C ... デザイン解説　Design Concept
D ... ロゴ　Logotype
E ... 店舗住所とウェブアドレス　Shop address & Web site address
F ... 制作スタッフ・クレジット　Creative Staff

✤ 制作スタッフクレジット　Creative Staff

A:　ショップ設計者　Architect Charge
AF:　建築設計事務所　Architectual Firm
CD:　クリエイティブ・ディレクター　Creative Director
AD:　アート・ディレクター　Art Director
LD:　ロゴ・デザイナー　Logo Designer
D:　デザイナー　Designer
P:　フォトグラファー　Photographer
I:　イラストレーター　Illustrator
CW:　コピーライター　Copywriter
DF:　グラフィックデザイン事務所　Design Firm
PR:　プロデューサー　Producer
SB:　作品提供者　Submitter

※上記以外の制作者呼称は省略せずに掲載しています。
　All other production titles are unabbreviated.

※本書に掲載されている店名、店舗写真、販促ツール、商品などは、すべて２００９年３月時点での情報になります。
　All in store-related information, including shop name, photography, promotional items and products are accurate as of March 2009.

※本書に掲載されている配布物は、既に終了しているものもありますので、ご了承ください。
　Please note that some paperworks are no longer deployed.

※作品提供者の意向によりデータの一部を記載していない場合があります。
　Please note that some credit information has been omitted at the request of the submitter.

※各企業に附随する、"株式会社、（株）"および"有限会社、（有）"は表記を省略させて頂きました。
　The "kabushiki gaisha" and "yugen gaisha" portions of all company name have been omitted.

New Food Shop Graphics

Cafes / Sweeteries

ネイン
Neyn

ドーナツといってもアメリカではなく、菓子の本場である、フランスを中心としたヨーロッパで菓子に使われる素材や手法を用いてドーナツを作ったら…という発想から生まれた。1つのロゴを作ってそれを全てに貼り付けるような、画一的なブランディング手法をとらず、一見矛盾するようなものも含めて緩やかに連係する複数のモチーフが合わさって1つの世界を表現している。

その世界とは、「ヨーロッパのキッチンにまつわる風景や思い出」。蝶や鳥、庭にひるがえる洗濯物など、キッチンにまつわる物語を紡ぎ出していく。

They're doughnuts but not the American kind. The idea was why not produce doughnuts with the ingredients and techniques for making sweets used in Europe, especially France, the center of the universe for all things sweet? Standard branding techniques such as one logo being used everywhere were avoided, and what has been expressed is one world that incorporates multiple motifs, some that at first glance seem contradictory, connecting seamlessly together. That world captures "scenes and memories from the kitchens of Europe," spinning a story about kitchens that involves butterflies and birds and laundry fluttering on the line in the garden.

Neyn

東京都港区赤坂5-4-8 1階
1F, 5-4-8 Akasaka, Minato-ku, Tokyo, JAPAN
http://www.neyn.com

AD: Simon Browning
Interior Design: 内海智行　Tomoyuki Utsumi
Chief Pâtissier: 森 由希子　Yukiko Mori
CL, SB: ネインジャパン　Neyn Japan Limited

Neyn

〒107-0052 東京都港区赤坂5-4-8 1F
1F 5-4-8 Akasaka, Minato-ku, Tokyo 107-0052
Tel 03-6459-1150 / Fax 03-6459-1151
www.neyn.com

Opening Hours

Weekdays 8:00—22:00
Saturdays 8:00—21:00
Sun / Holidays 9:00—20:00

Neyn

〒107-0052 東京都港区赤坂5-4-8 1F
1F 5-4-8 Akasaka, Minato-ku, Tokyo 107-0052
Tel 03-6459-1150 / Fax 03-6459-1151
www.neyn.com

Opening Hours
Weekdays 8:00—22:00
Saturdays 8:00—21:00
Sun / Holidays 9:00—20:00

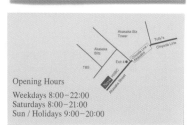

Sticker

Neyn / handmade

ドーナツ / Doughnuts

プレーン / Plain	230
ガトーショコラ / Gâteau Chocolat	260
キャラメルクロッカン / Caramel Croquant	260
ベリールージュ / Berry Rouge	260
ホワイトフィグ / White Figue	260
ココア / Cocoa	270
フロマージュ / Fromage	270
抹茶あん / Green Tea Azuki	270
ケークオフリュイ / Cake Aux Fruits	280
ネインモンブラン / Neyn Mont Blanc	300

温かい飲み物 / Hot Drinks

コーヒー / Coffee
カフェラテ / Caffè Latte
カフェモカ / Caffè Mocha

紅茶 / Tea
ミントブレンド / Mint Blend
カモミールブレンド / Camomile Blend
ローズヒップブレンド / Rose Hip Blend
ロイヤルミルクティー / Royal Milk Tea

ホットミルク / Hot Milk
ホットチョコレート / Hot Chocolate

冷たい飲み物 / Cold Drinks

アイスコーヒー / Iced Coffee
アイスカフェラテ / Iced Caffè Latte
アイスカフェモカ / Iced Caffè Mocha
アイスティー / Iced Tea

ミルク / Milk
チョコレートドリンク / Chocolate Drink

コーラ / ダイエットコーラ / Coke / Diet Coke
ジンジャーエール / Ginger Ale
オレンジジュース / Orange Juice
グレープフルーツジュース / Grapefruit Juice

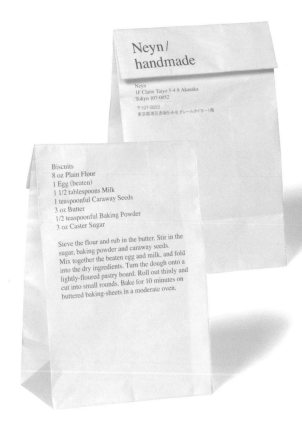

Biscuits
8 oz Plain Flour
1 Egg (beaten)
1 1/2 tablespoons Milk
1 teaspoonful Caraway Seeds
3 oz Butter
1/2 teaspoonful Baking Powder
3 oz Caster Sugar

Sieve the flour and rub in the butter. Stir in the
sugar, baking powder and caraway seeds.
Mix together the beaten egg and milk, and fold
into the dry ingredients. Turn the dough onto a
lightly-floured pastry board. Roll out thinly and
cut into small rounds. Bake for 10 minutes on
buttered baking-sheets in a moderate oven.

1 / Coot
2 / Blue Tit
3 / Fieldfare
4 / Ring Ouzle
5 / Cockerel
6 / Nuthatch
7 / Mallard
8 / Domestic Goose
9 / Mute Swan
10 / Avocet
11 / Magpie
12 / House Martin
13 / Purple Gallinule
14 / Whimbrel
15 / Horned Lark
16 / Heron
17 / Little Grebe
18 / Blackcap
19 / Blackbird
20 / Lesser Spotted Woodpecker
21 / Hummingbird

Novelty

Here and there

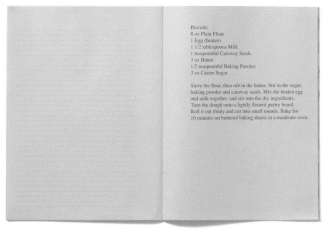

Biscuits
8 oz Plain Flour
1 Egg (beaten)
1 1/2 tablespoons Milk
1 teaspoonful Caraway Seeds
3 oz Butter
1/2 teaspoonful Baking Powder
3 oz Castor Sugar

Sieve the flour, then rub in the butter. Stir in the sugar,
baking powder and caraway seeds. Mix the beaten egg
and milk together, and stir into the dry ingredients.
Turn the dough onto a lightly floured pastry board.
Roll it out thinly and cut into small rounds. Bake for
10 minutes on buttered baking sheets in a moderate oven.

Over the fence and into the field

Postcards

カップケーキ専門店

Cupcake Shop

フェアリーケーキフェア
Fairycake Fair

イギリスの家庭で受け継がれてきた伝統的なカップケーキを、季節の素材とおいしい組合せ、ケーキ感覚のデコレーションで仕上げる、新しいカタチのカップケーキ専門店。ロゴ、パッケージも昔からロンドンの日常生活にとけ込む、あたたかな中性的なイメージで、イギリスの60年代の小説にでてくるような構想で作り上げた。

A new type of specialty cupcake store that produces the traditional cup cakes that have been part of British family life for generations, made with seasonal ingredients and in delicious combinations, and decorated in the same way as cakes. Both the logo and packaging have a warm, neutral image of everyday life of London in the old days with a design straight out of a British novel from the '60s.

Fairycake Fair
and milk tea.

東京都千代田区丸の内1-9-1
JR東日本東京駅構内B1
B1 East Japan Railway Tokyo Station,
1-9-1, Marunouchi, Chiyoda-ku, Tokyo,
JAPAN
http://www.fairycake.jp

A: 刑部 茂（刑部デザイン）
Shigeru Gyobu（Gyobu Design）
CD: 杉浦 幸　Yuki Sugiura／いがらしろみ
Romi Igarashi／後藤国弘　Kunihiro Goto
AD, LD: 今井クミ　Kumi Imai
D: 塩澤偉史　Yoshifumi Shiozawa／多賀健史
Takeshi Taga／小田嶋暁子　Akiko Odashima／
佐藤香佳　Kasumi Sato（CPCenter）
P: 新居明子　Akiko Arai
DF, SB: アピスラボラトリー
Apis Laboratory Inc.

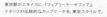

Balencia dolce vita

神戸北野のブライダル施設solaにある飲食店。額縁を随所に使用した店舗イメージにあわせて、高級感のある額縁で構成した。スペインらしい大胆な曲線に高級店としての繊細さをプラスしている。

A restaurant inside the sola wedding facility in Kitano, Kobe. In line with the restaurant's image with its plentiful use of picture frames, the graphics were built around a high-quality picture frame. The restaurant is a combination of typically Spanish bold curves and the subtlety of a high-end restaurant.

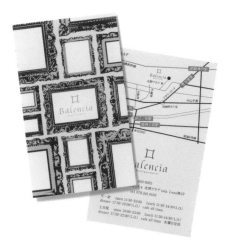

Flyer

兵庫県神戸市中央区北野町1-5-4
北野クラブsola Luna棟1F
1F, 1-5-4, Kitano-machi, Chuo-ku,
Kobe-city, Hyogo, JAPAN
http://www.balencia.jp/

A: カフェ　Cafe co.／森井良幸　Yoshiyuki Morii
CD: 金谷 勉　Tsutomu Kanaya
AD: 二口 勤　Tsutomu Futakuchi
D, LD: 千星健夫
Takeo Chiboshi（Menu book, Plate）
D: 植山佳則
Yoshinori Ueyama（Shopping bag, Shop card）
CL: バレンシア　Balencia
SB: セメントプロデュースデザイン
CEMENT PRODUCE DESIGN

Roll Cake Shop

デザートナンバーイチ
ロールケーキ

Dessert No.1 Roll Cake

「線と面」をキーワードに生んだスクエアブルな空間に、珪藻土・無垢の木・真鍮など「質感とその変化」を前提とした素材の集積と編集により、視覚的な「手触り感」をうながした。そこに地元の歴史が育んだ横浜家具という技術と知恵を濃縮し活かしたデザイントーンを描き、空間に品性と落ち着きを与えた。「ローカリティという力」と向き合うこと、そのものが全体における思想となっている。

"Line and plane" as keys words give rise to a geometric space in which the compilation and integration of the material qualities of earthen plaster, untreated wood, bronze, etc. and the changes they undergo trigger a visual sense of tactility. The design tone created by giving full play to local techniques and wisdom known as Yokohama furniture adds character and serenity to the space. A hard look at the "power of locality" resulted in it forming the overall idea.

Dessert No.1 Roll Cake

神奈川県横浜市中区山下町108-105
108-105, Yamashita-cho, Naka-ku,
Yokohama-city, Kanagawa, JAPAN
http://www.e-loupe.jp

AF: 神興建設　Shinkou Kensetsu Inc.
CD, AD, D, LD, Space Designer: 成澤 豪
Go Narisawa
D: 成澤宏美　Hiromi Narisawa
Production of fixtures & fittings 什器制作：
蓮華草元町工房　Rengeso Motomachikobo, Inc.
Sign Making 看板制作：杉山製作所
Sugiyama Seisakusho Co., Ltd.
DF, SB: なかよし図工室
Nakayoshi Zukoushitsu, Inc.
CL: ルーペ　Loupe Corporation

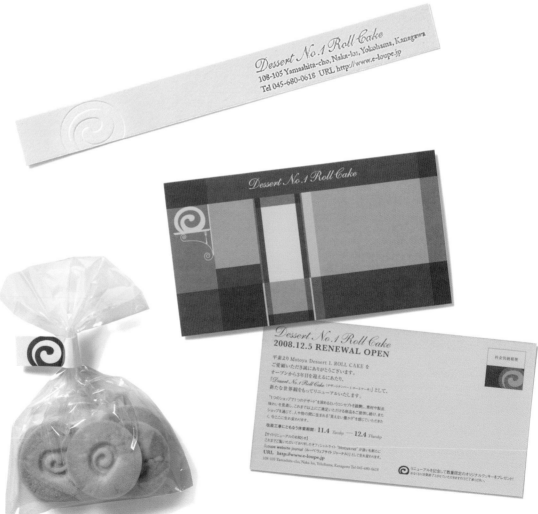

Floor Mat

ドーナツカフェ

Doughnut Café

andonand

「大人のミスド」をコンセプトにミスタ
ードーナツが展開するドーナツカフェ。
ミッドセンチュリーモダンな店内に緑
を配置しボサノバを流す、その中で素
材にこだわったドーナツとコーヒーを
提供している。都会のビジネスパーソン
が忙しい日常に一息つける空間「アーバ
ンオアシス」を演出。

A doughnut café developed by Mister
Donut, based on the concept of a "Mister
Donut for grown-ups." It offers
doughnuts and coffee made from the best
ingredients in a mid-century modern
interior filled with greenery and bossa
nova music. The space is an "urban oasis,"
a place for busy city business people to
take a breather.

東京都渋谷区宇田川町2-1
2-1, Udagawa-cho, Shibuya-ku, Tokyo,
JAPAN
http://www.andonand.jp

AD: 伊藤健一　Kenichi Ito
D: 千葉 妙　Tae Chiba
P: 高田浩行　Hiroyuki Takada
Space Designer: ディー・ファイン　D-Fine
DF: 花積デザイン事務所
HANAZUMI Design OFFICE
CL, SB: ダスキン　DUSKIN CO., LTD.

Coaster

What's andonand?

アンドナンドは、
おいしいものに敏感な大人のための、ドーナツカフェです。
プレミアムなおいしさを追求した、ドーナツを中心に
次世代のカフェメニューを取り揃えています。
もちろん、コーヒーにもこだわっています。

アンドナンドの店名は、
ドーナツを握手をする国際を形容する「andonand」と
日本語の「あであん」からなる造語です。
いつも、あなたのそばに「and」口常着がいたい。
アンドナンドは、お客さまの毎日の楽しさの変化を
お店でごもてなしています。

そして、私たちがつくりたかった
本当の贅沢をこころよく、ぜひ、お楽しみください。

http://www.andonand.jp

Donut ドーナツへのこだわりは、誰にも負けない。

Patisserie Donut Espresso Affogato

Granite Chou Caramel Custard

Menu

プレミアムドーナツ
Premium Donut
¥250

クラシックチョコレートドーナツ
Classic Chocolate Donut
¥180

クラシックドーナツ
Classic Donut
¥180

グラニットチュー
Granite Chou
¥230

マフィン
Muffin
¥230

ブルーベリーチーズ
Blueberry Cheese

メープルアーモンド
Maple Almond

リッチショコラ
Rich Chocolate

黒糖黒糖
Black Yarbrae Brown Sugar
¥230

ナッツ
Chocolate

レモンティー
Lemon Tea

シナモン
Cinnamon

アップルシナモン
Apple Cinnamon

ミックスベリー
Mixed Berries

カスタードアーモンド
Custard Almond

パティスリードーナツ
Patisserie Donut
¥400

チョコ＆ココナッツ
Chocolate & Cocoa

抹茶黒糖
Green Tea Black Yarbrae

クランベリーアーモンド
Cranberry Almond

サンドウィッチ
Sandwich　各種　¥420

Drink Menu

Coffee

アンドナンド ブレンドコーヒー　andonand Blend Coffee	¥300	¥350
アンドナンド ブレンドコーヒー マイルド　andonand Blend Coffee Mild	¥300	¥350
アイスコーヒー　Iced Coffee	¥300	¥350

Espresso

アンドナンドラテ　andonand Latte Hot / cold	¥320	¥370
ラズベリーモカ　Raspberry Mocha Hot / cold	¥380	¥430
カフェアメリカーノ　Caffè Americano	¥320	
ソイラテ　Soy Latte Hot / cold	¥360	¥410
キャラメルラテ　Caramel Latte Hot / cold	¥360	¥410
カフェモカ　Caffè Mocha Hot / cold	¥360	¥410
エスプレッソ　Espresso	¥300	¥350
ショット追加　Additional shot of Espresso	+50	
ホイップ追加　Additional Whipped Cream	+50	
低脂肪乳への変更　Low-fat milk available for no-extra-charge	+0	

Tea & Juice

チャイ　Chai Hot / cold	¥320
アイスミルクティー　Iced Milk Tea Hot / cold	¥320
オレンジジュース　Orange Juice	¥320
パイナップルジュース　Pineapple Juice	¥320
マンゴージュース　Mango Juice	¥320

Donafrozen

キャラメル ナナフローズン　Caramel Donafrozen	¥420
セサミオレ ドナフローズン　Mochifano Donafrozen	¥420
ミックスベリー ナナフローズン　Mixed Berries Donafrozen	¥420
マンゴー ナナフローズン　Mango Donafrozen	¥420

Soup

海老とトマトのクリームスープ　Cream Soup of Lobster and Tomato	¥420
五穀入りチキンベジタブルスープ　Green Vegetable Soup with Five Grains	¥420

2008.11.01 start

new face!

プレミアムドーナツ
チョコクランベリー
Premium Donut / Chocolate Cranberry
¥250

クラシックドーナツ
グランデマロン
Classic Donut / Blanch & Chestnut Cream
¥230

マフィン
オレンジチョコ
Orange Muffin
¥230

マロンラテ
Chestnut Latte　Hot / cold

R ¥360　L ¥410

ADVANCE ORDER START!

Order Sheet

予約販売受付中

ADVANCE ORDER

予約販売受付中

POT SERVICE

ドリンクポット
サービス

Fax：03-6215-6566

アンドナンド ペディ宿営店

Posters

P.O.P

スウィート・ソウル・スウィーツ

Sweet Soul Sweets

手作り100種類マフィン店。「マフィンを食べた人に（おいしい・うれしい）元気のパワー（＝生命力）を提供する」というコンセプトをV.Iを中心に各ツールに反映させた。伝統を感じられるデザインを用いながらも、マフィンの持つ魅力（生命力のパワー）を動植物のモチーフで表わし、さりげなく各ツールに入れている。また、店主の幼少時代の記憶の中にある、イギリスの家庭で行われる裏庭のティータイムの空気感を演出するため、ショーケースは、石・木・グリーン・陶器を用い、地下の空間でも風・光・緑が感じられる店舗空間を目指した。

A shop with 100 kinds of handmade muffins. Each of the tools based around the visual identity reflects the concept of "muffins that offer vitality to the people who eat them (delicious, happy). Although the design feels traditional, the charm (vitality) that muffins hold was expressed with a plant and animal motif and casually incorporated into each of the tools. The aim was to create a store space that incorporated air, light and greenery even in basement locations, using showcases made from stone, wood, green and ceramic to create an atmosphere of teatime in the back garden of a British home, a childhood memory of the store's owner.

SWEET SOUL SWEETS®
100 KINDS OF SOULFUL MUFFINS

東京都中央区銀座3-2-1
プランタン銀座B2F
PRINTEMPS GINZA 3-2-1, Ginza,
Chuo-ku, Tokyo, JAPAN
http://sweetsoulsweets.com

CD, AD, D, LD: 川崎恵美　Emi Kawasaki
Space Designer: 増田健太　Kenta Masuda
AF, DF, SB: アンデザイン　andesign. co., ltd.
CL: 甘心　amagocoro

Chocolatier

ショコラティエ パレ ド オール
CHOCOLATIER PALET D'OR

取り扱う商品と店舗コンセプトを考慮
し、シェフが全体のデザインイメージを
仕上げ、設計者とのミーティングによっ
て完成した図面から、乃村工藝社が施
工して仕上げた。

The chef was responsible for the overall
design image that took account of the
products on sale and the store concept,
and based on the drawings that were
finalized after meetings with the designer,
Nomura Kōgei completed the
construction work.

カフェ／スウィーツ　Cafes / Sweeteries

東京都千代田区丸の内1-5-1
新丸の内ビルディング1F
1F, 1-5-1, Marunouchi, Chiyoda-ku,
Tokyo, JAPAN
http://www.palet-dor.com

A, D: 宮城一也　Kazuya Miyagi
CD, AD, SpaceDesigner: 三枝俊介
Shunsuke Saegusa
AF: 乃村工藝社　Nomura-Kōgei
LD: 雨宮深雪　Miyuki Amemiya
P: 細野幸人　Yukino Hosono
DF: シマダデザイン　Shimada Design
CL, SB: ロジアスetデューン
L'oasis et Dune Co., Ltd.

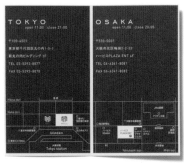

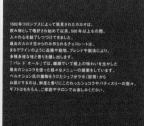

Sticker

チョコレートブラウニー専門店

Chocolate Brownie Shop

コート・クール
côte cour

ジュエリーショップのような外観だが、店内はシャンパンゴールドを基調とした落ち着いた雰囲気。ブラウニーをイメージしたレンガの壁にショーケースはレザー張り。オリエンタルなムードを演出するためブラウニーは焼きものを思わせる大理石にのせてディスプレイしている。コンセプトがオリエンタルであるため、制服や紙袋には和を取り入れている。

From the outside it appears to be a jewelry store, but the relaxed ambience inside is created by champagne gold. The walls are brick in the image of a brownie and the showcases are upholstered in leather. To create an Oriental mood, the brownies are displayed on marble reminiscent of ceramic ware. Because the concept is Oriental, a Japanese style has been incorporated into the uniforms and paper bags.

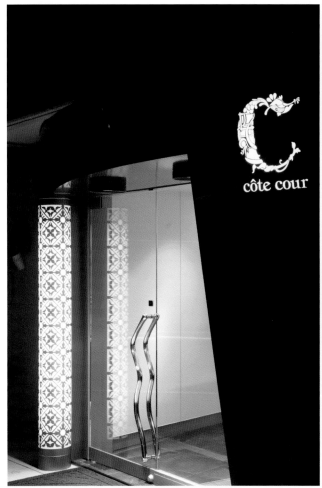

東京都渋谷区東 3-9-40
3-9-40, Higashi, Shibuya-ku, Tokyo, JAPAN
http://www.cotecour.jp

CL, SB: côte cour

〒150-0013
東京都渋谷区東 3-9-40
TEL:03-5464-3535
www.cotecour.jp

デルレイ カフェ＆
ショコラティエ
DEL REY Café & Chocolatier

「食を通じて、ゲストに特別な経験をしていただく」がコンセプト。カフェコーナーはプラチナカラーと白で統一されたシンプルモダンな内装。デザインされたショコラを宝石に見立て、1粒ずつ美しくディスプレイ。パッケージはマットな白とメタリックシルバーを基調に、宝石や香水のための箱の印象で。微妙なカーブで面をとり、シンプルかつ気品ある表情に仕上げ、ブランドイメージを体現した。

The concept was "offer your guests a special experience through food." The café corner has a simple modern interior brought together with platinum colors and white. To have customers choose the beautifully designed chocolates much as they would jewelry, each one is exquisitely displayed. The matte white and metallic silver packaging evokes an image of boxes for precious stones and perfume. Delicately curved, they are simple yet graceful, embodying the brand image.

Café & Chocolatier

東京都渋谷区神宮前 4-12-10
表参道ヒルズ本館 3F
3F, 4-12-10 Jingumae, Shibuya-Ku,
Tokyo, JAPAN
http://www.delrey.co.jp/

CL, SB: ル・ショコラ・デュ・ディアマン
Le Chocolat Du Diamant
D: 北川一成　Issei Kitagawa（GRAPH）
Space Designer: 河内 聡（カサレ・アソシエイツ）
Kawauchi Satoshi（Casale Associates）

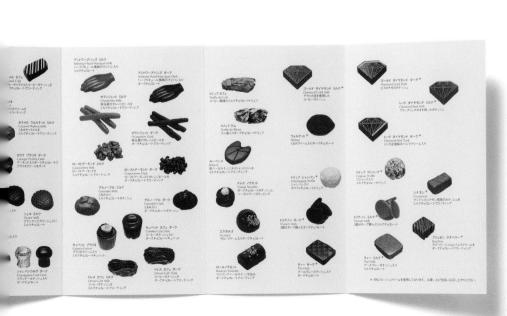

ハーブス 栄本店
HARBS

フレッシュネスとハンドメイドを追求し
たフレッシュケーキ＆カフェ。素材その
ままの美味しさを表現する商品コンセ
プトを軸に、シンプルな中にも柔らかさ
と力強さを備えたグラフィックでオリジ
ナリティを打ち出している。

A cake shop and café with a focus on
freshness and the hand made. In keeping
with the shop's concept of products that
emphasize the natural goodness of their
ingredients, the graphics, in their
simplicity, elicit originality by possessing
both softness and strength.

愛知県名古屋市中区錦3-6-17
セントラルパークビル 2F
2F, 3-6-17 Nishiki, Naka-ku,
Nagoya-city, Aichi, JAPAN
http://www.harbs.co.jp

A, AF: ワクト　WACT Co., Ltd.
CD, AD, D, LD, SB: 重光　SHIGEMITSU., LTD

DRINK

Tea

SPECIAL CAKE

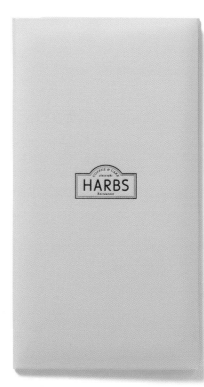

Gift Catalog

FRESH GIFT

Gerateria

イタリアンジェラート ロノ
Italian gelato RONO

ジェラートの素材の色を際立たせるために、空間をモノトーンで統一。可能な限り整理された空間に描かれたモールディング模様が鏡張りの壁とあいまって、不思議な浮遊感を生み出している。パッケージも空間のイメージを継承したデザインとし、一貫したブランディングを心がけている。

The space was brought together in a monotone to highlight the colors of the gelati ingredients. The molding pattern drawn on the cleanest of spaces coupled with the mirror-covered walls produces a strange floating feeling. The packaging design incorporates the image for the space, ever mindful of coherent branding.

RONO
Italian gelato

愛知県日進市赤池2-606 川村ビル1F
1F, 2-606 Akaike, Nisshin-city, Aichi, JAPAN

A: 三宅博之　Hiroyuki Miyake
CD: 村井浩起　Hiroki Murai
LD: 臼井康文　Yasufumi Usui
DF: 三宅博之デザインオフィス
Hiroyuki Miyake Design Office.
Construction: オカ巧芸　Oka Kougei
CL, SB: シンスケ　SHINSUKE

ラ・ヴィ・アン・ローズ
LA VIE EN ROSE

「いきなり老舗」をコンセプトに制作。路地に入った知る人ぞ知る場所を店舗位置としてセレクトし、店内は鮮やかなお菓子を引き立たせるためにホワイトを基調とした空間を演出している。グラフィックツールにはイベントごとにサブカラーを使用するなど季節感を感じられるようにした。

Produced with the concept "all of a sudden a long-established store." The store, located in a back street and known by people "in the know," has a white interior to make the colorful sweets stand out. The change of season is celebrated by, among other things, using sub-colors in the graphic tools for each seasonal event.

LA VIE EN ROSE
PATISSERIE FUKUOKA

福岡県福岡市博多区住吉4-3-2, 1F
1F, 4-3-2, Sumiyoshi, Hakata-ku,
Fukuoka-city, Fukuoka, JAPAN

A: 福田哲也　Tetsuya Fukuda
AF: アーキタンツ　ARCHITANZ
AD, D, DF, SB: ディーライト　DEELGHTS
P: 石井紀久　Toshihisa Ishii

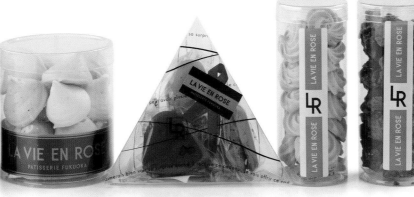

ラ ブティック ドゥ ジョエル・ロブション

六本木ヒルズ店

LA BOUTIQUE de Joël
Robuchon Roppongi Hills

「厳選した素材本来の価値を最大限に
活かす」というジョエル・ロブション氏
の料理哲学「シンプル・フレンチ」に基
づき、職人が丁寧に手作りしたパンや
スウィーツ、コンフィチュール等を販売
するテイクアウト専門店。赤と黒を基調
にした店内同様、ツール類も赤と黒を
使用。ピエール・イヴ・ロション氏デザ
インのロゴを、アートディレクター渡邊
かをる氏の手により、ギフトBOX、ショ
ッパーにデザインした。

A specialty takeaway store that sells bread,
sweets and jam among other things,
handmade by a craftsman and based on
the "Simply French" cooking philosophy
of Joël Robuchon that maximizes the
essential value of carefully selected
ingredients. The same red and black used
for the store interior with base colors of
red and black were used for the tools also.
The logo was designed by Pierre Yves
Rochon and the gift box and shopper by
art director, Kaoru Watanabe.

東京都港区六本木6-10-1
六本木ヒルズヒルサイド2F
2F, 6-10-1, Roppongi, Minato-ku, Tokyo,
JAPAN
http://www.robuchon.jp/

A, LD: Pierre Yves Rochon
AF: アフタヌーンソサエティ
AFTERNOON SOCIETY Inc.
Total Producer: Joël Robuchon
AD: 渡邊かをる Kaoru Watanabe
SB: アンティル ANTIL

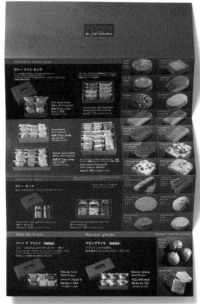

紅茶専門店

Tea House

コヴェントガーデン
COVENT GARDEN

英国田舎風の紅茶店で、50種類の紅茶と熱々のパンケーキを提供する。COVENT GARDEN とはロンドンのセントラルにある地区で、映画「マイ・フェア・レディ」でオードリー演じる花売り娘イライザが働いていた、当時の建物の一部が残っていたり、新旧が混在する面白い地区。これをヒントに、こげ茶の田舎風イメージとロンドンのモダンできれいな白という対照的な部分が一体化された空間を作った。

A rustic British tea shop offering 50 kinds of tea and piping hot pancakes. Convent Garden, an area in the center of London, is the place where flower girl Eliza Doolittle (played by Audrey Hepburn in the film My Fair Lady) worked. Some of the buildings from that time are still standing. It is a vibrant area where the new and the old coexist.
Based thereupon, a unified space has been created from the contrast between a dark brown rustic image and the clean white of London Modern.

Tea House

COVENT GARDEN

神奈川県横浜市西区南幸 2-13
東急ハンズ 2F
2A Floor, 2-13, Minamisaiwai, Nishi-ku,
Yokohama-shi, Kanagawa, JAPAN

A: キュール　CUEL／山田 寛　Hiroshi Yamada
／ハギワラトシコ　Toshiko Hagiwara
LD: レスパース　L'espace
SB: 宮本ビル　MiyamotoBldg.

Menu

コンフィチュール専門店

Confiturier

ベルベリー

Belberry

店のコンセプトは「常軌を逸した存在感」。そのシンボル的存在として、アイキャッチになる釣り下がりのペンダント照明のニットシャンデリアをニットデザイナーのモキリーに制作を依頼。そのシャンデリアを引き立てるよう、下にはろくろで回転したような印象のモールディングを施した木製の什器を配した。店の中央にある高い天井までそびえるセラーには、コンフィチュールがずらりと並ぶ。パッケージは、本国でもテーマカラーの赤と白のコントラスト。

The shop's concept is "eccentric presence." Knit designer Mokely was asked to produce the eye-catching pendant-style knitted chandelier as a symbol of that presence. To set off the chandelier, a wooden display case with molding that appeared to have been turned on a lathe was positioned below it. Jams are displayed on a wine rack that rises from to the ceiling at the high-ceilinged center of the space. The packaging features the same contrasting theme colors of red and white as the main store in Belgium.

MAÎTRE CONFITURIER
Est. 1956 Belgium

東京都港区赤坂9-7-4
東京ミッドタウンガレリア B1F
B1F, 9-7-4 Akasaka, Minato-ku, Tokyo, JAPAN
http://www.belberry.jp/

CL, SB: ル・ショコラ・デュ・ディアマン
Le chocolat du diamant
Space Designer: 上垣内泰輔（丹青社）
Taisuke Kamigaichi（TANSEISHA）
Artist: Mokely

Flyers

表参道シュークリング
OMOTESANDO Choux Cring

リング状のシュー生地にさまざまなフレーバーのクリームを詰めた新スウィーツ "Choux Cring（シュークリング）" 専門店。ブラウンとホワイトを基調に、ピンクの文字を上面に配置した "シック" と "かわいらしさ" を併せ持つイメージのパッケージデザインを打ち出した。

A specialty store offering a new type of sweet, the Choux Cring, made from "choux" pastry in the shape of a ring and filled with cream in a variety of flavors. The packaging design features a combination of chic and cute with pink type on the front, on top of basic tones of brown and white.

東京都港区北青山 3-6-12
表参道駅　Echika 表参道
Echika Omotesando, Omotesando
Station, 3-6-12, Kita-Aoyama
Minato-ku, Tokyo, JAPAN
http://www.global-dining.com/

D: 佐久間美智夫　Michio Sakuma
CL, SB: グローバルダイニング
Global-Dining, Inc.

ミエルドーナツ
MIEL DONUT

初めて大阪から東京に進出した際に、赤いテーマカラーを取り入れた。エコバッグ、サーモカップ、マグカップなどのグッズの売上金の一部をセーブザチルドレンに寄付しているほか、持ち帰りの箱が不要という場合はお客さまに代わってNPOにポリオワクチンを寄贈している。

The red theme color was incorporated when the Osaka-based store opened branches in Tokyo. As well as contributing a part of the proceeds from the sale of items such as eco-bags, thermo cups and mugs to Save the Children, when customers forgo a box in which to take away their purchases, a polio vaccine is donated to an NPO on their behalf.

miel
BAKED DONUT

Sticker

東京都中央区銀座6-12-1
6-12-1 Ginza, Chuo-ku, Tokyo, JAPAN
http://www.miel-donut.com

CL, SB: ミエル　MIEL

Menu

チョコレート専門店

Chocolatier

バニラシュガー
vanilla sugar

コンセプトは「女性を元気にする」チョコレート。「楽しい」「かわいい」「きれい」「おいしい」と素直に感じてもらえるような店・商品づくりを目指した。カラーは、白・水色・シルバーの3色を基調に、シンプルで少し無機質に見せながらも、ショコラドールをよく見たときの可愛さや、食べた時のおいしさとのよい意味でのギャップを感じてもらえたらと思っている。

The concept was "chocolate that cheers women up." The objective was to create products and a shop environment that would be thought "fun", "adorable", "beautiful" and "delicious." The three basic colors are white, light blue and silver, and although simple with a slightly inorganic quality, the idea was to make customers sense the gap–in a positive way–between that and the cuteness felt when looking at the chocolate doll, and delicious taste when you ate it.

vanilla sugar

東京都中央区銀座3-2-1
プランタン銀座B2F
B2F Printemps Ginza, 3-2-1 Ginza, Chuo-ku, Tokyo, JAPAN
http://www.vanillasugar.jp/

CD: 八木克尚　Katsuhisa Yagi
AD: 菅原三恵子　Mieko Sugawara
LD: 富士亜希　Aki Fuji（PECCIA Co.Ltd.）
SB: チョコレートデザイン
CHOCOLATE DESIGN COMPANY

Message Card

If you have something fun, cute, lovely, and delicious in everyday life your body and mind will be cheered up.

Wrapping paper

パパブブレ
papabubble

スペインのバルセロナが本店のキャンディー専門店。店舗デザインやアンティークを使用したインテリアは本店と同じMr.BONESによるもの。キャンディーの輝きやカラフルさを生かすため、商品パッケージやラッピングはシンプルに。クリスマスなど、年に数回発売される限定ラベルは、複数のデザイナーにより独特な世界観を表現した仕上がりになっている。

A specialty candy store originating in the Spanish city of Barcelona. The store's interior design and the use of antiques are by Mr. BONES, the same as for the main store. The product packaging and the wrapping were kept simple to highlight the sparkling colors of the candy. The limited edition candy put on sale several times a year such as at Christmas express the unique worldview of a number of designers.

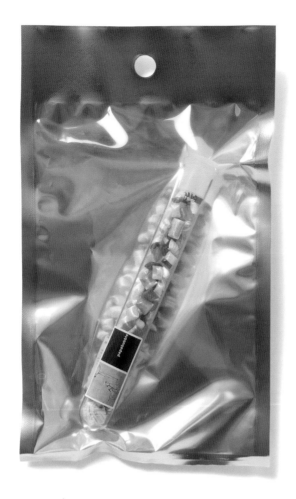

東京都中野区新井1-15-13
1-15-13, Arai, Nakano-ku, Tokyo, JAPAN
http://www.papabubble.com

A: Mr. BONES
AD: Tommy & Christopher
Sticker Designer: Rachel Hooper／Fiona Ryan
SB: カンノ　Kanno

papabubble
caramels artesans

Tel/Fax 03 5343 1286
Arai 1-15-13 Nakano Tokyo

www.papabubble.com

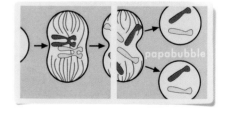

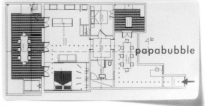

Stickers

Stickers

Entertainment Ice Cream Shop

コールド・ストーン・クリーマリー
Cold Stone Creamery

アイスクリームとミックスイン（フルーツ・ナッツ等）を−9℃に冷やした石の上で混ぜ合わせて提供する、アメリカ発のエンターテインメント・アイスクリームショップ。"Make People Happy"をモットーに、豊富なアイスクリームとミックスインの種類、目の前で作られる自分だけの組み合わせ、クルーの歌やおもてなしと、すべての瞬間を楽しめるハッピークリーマリー体験を提供している。

An entertainment-style ice cream shop originating in the United States, where the ice-cream and "mix-ins" such as fruits and nuts are mixed together on a frozen granite stone (-9℃). With the motto "Make People Happy," it offers a "happy creamery experience" with an abundant range of ice cream flavors and mix-ins, ice cream that is made right in front of you, and the friendly service of the servers who sing for the customers.

東京都新宿区新宿3-38-1
ルミネエスト新宿店 8F
8F LUMINE EST, 3-38-1 Shinjuku,
Shinjuku-ku, Tokyo, JAPAN
http://www.coldstonecreamery.co.jp

A: 平川尚巳　Naomi Hirakawa
AF: ナイツ・アンド・カンパニー
Nyts & Co. Ltd.
CD, CW: 大友美有紀　Miyuki Otomo
AD, D: 岡本 学　Manabu Okamoto
D: 赤羽美和　Miwa Akabane
PR: 藤田 隆　Takashi Fujita／常木宏之
Hiroyuki Tsuneki
DF, SB: サン・アド　SUN-AD Co. Ltd

DM

Strawberry Shortcake Serenade

Happy Creamery Experience!

COLD STONE CREAMERY

Cookie Mixture

Happy Creamery Experience!

COLD STONE CREAMERY

Apple Pie A La Cold Stone

Happy Creamery Experience!

COLD STONE CREAMERY

Chocolate Devotion

Happy Creamery Experience!

COLD STONE CREAMERY

At the Cocoa Banana Cabana

Happy Creamery Experience!

COLD STONE CREAMERY

Cards

Taste of Romance

クリスマスの恋人たちに贈る
上質なデザート、ミルフィーユ。
サクッとした食感と濃厚なおいしさのハーモニーが
極上の贅沢な時間を演出します。

Like It ￥480 *Love It* ￥610 *Gotta Have It* ￥930
Waffle Cone ￥60 *Waffle Bowl* ￥60
Chocolate Waffle Cone ￥120 *Chocolate Waffle Bowl* ￥120

✻ Winter Mille-Feuille Wishes ✻
ウィンター ミルフィーユ ウィッシィズ
※カスタードアイスクリーム
ストロベリー、パイ

COOLLY'S evolution!

アイスでもないドリンクでもない
今までにないおいしさの「クーリーズ」に、
新しい愉しみが増えました。
第2弾フローズンリッチミルクベース登場です。

Create Your Own クリエイト ユア オウン

組み合わせは無限大。あなたのチョイスで、世界にひとつだけのオリジナルのおいしさをつくってください。

◯ Ice Cream Flavors アイスクリーム

sweet cream スイートクリーム	chocolate チョコレート	banana バナナ	mint ミント	french vanilla フレンチバニラ
coffee コーヒー	white chocolate ホワイトチョコレート	cheesecake チーズケーキ	strawberry ストロベリー	mango マンゴ
green tea グリーンティー				

◯ Mix Ins ミックスイン

Fruits フルーツ	Chocolate チョコレート	Nuts ナッツ	Cakes & Candies 菓子類	Topping & Misc. ソース類
banana バナナ	chocolate chips チョコレートチップ	roasted almonds ローストアーモンド	yellow cake スポンジケーキ	peanut butter ピーナッツバター
strawberries ストロベリー	white chocolate chips ホワイトチョコレートチップ	pecans ピーカンナッツ	brownie ブラウニー	whipped topping ホイップクリーム
blueberries ブルーベリー	rainbow sprinkle レインボー スプレンクル	pistachios ピスタチオ	graham pie crust グラハムパイクラスト	chocolate chips チョコレートチップ

COOLLY'S クーリーズ

アイスでもないドリンクでもない新ジャンルのおいしさ。
今までにないデザート体験をお楽しみいただけます。
すっきりおいしいフローズンヨーグルトベースと
濃厚なおいしさのフローズンリッチミルクベース。
気分に合わせてお選びください。

ONE SIZE ￥600

Frozen Yogurt Base フローズンヨーグルトベース

Frozen Rich Milk Base フローズンリッチミルクベース

Cold Stone Creations コールドストーン クリエーション

アメリカで長く愛されてきた組み合わせです。あなたのお気に入りを見つけてください。さあ、ハッピークリーマリー体験の始まりです。

COLD STONE CREAMERY

How to order ご注文方法

1 メニューを選んでください。

2 食べるスタイルを選んでください。
  Like It ￥480 *Love It* ￥610 *Gotta Have It* ￥930

3 食べるスタイルを選んでください。
  +￥60 +￥120 +￥60 +￥120

Take Out
Cold Stone Creations Pint ￥1,330

Menu

www.coldstonecreamery.

COLD STONE CREAMERY

COLD STONE CREAMERY

COLD STONE CREAMERY

COLD STONE CREAMERY

洋菓子店

Cake Shop

王様からのご褒美 有楽町店
Ousama Karano gohobi

お客様が「小さな贅沢」と「大いなる満足」を感じられるよう原料に「ロイヤル食材」「ブランド食材」を贅沢に使用。コンセプトは「大人の贅沢」。ロゴ、カラー、包材、店舗デザインは「スタイリッシュ&ゴージャス」に統一し「特別な日＝晴れの日」にも対応できるイメージで製作を行っている。

Generous use of royal and brand ingredients offering customers "a little luxury" and "great satisfaction." The concept is "luxury for adults." The logo, color palette, wrapping materials, and store design have been unified "stylishly and gorgeously" around an image of a place that also caters to "special days and formal occasions."

東京都千代田区有楽町1-11-1
東京メトロ有楽町線有楽町駅構内
1-11-1, Yuraku-cho, Chiyoda-ku, Tokyo, JAPAN
http://www.ousama-sweets.com

A: スケール　scale
CD: オフィス・ビー　OFFICE B
SB: さかえ屋　Sakaeya Co.,Ltd

Shop Card

Cheese Cakes

Chocolate Box

ロールケーキ専門店

Roll Cake Shop

アリンコ 東京ステーション
ARINCO TOKYO STATION

小麦粉や卵、砂糖、バニラビーンズなど
本物のシンプルな素材と味わいをコン
セプトにしているロールケーキ専門店。
自然の甘さに反応するアリのキャラク
ターをモチーフとした。その一度見たら
忘れられない表情が、老若男女を問わ
ず広い客層の心をとらえている。

A specialty sponge roll cake store, the
concept of which is simple, authentic
ingredients (flour, eggs, sugar, and vanilla
beans) and flavor. The motif is an ant
character who reacts to the natural
sweetness. His once-seen-never-forgotten
facial expression captured the hearts of a
range of customers of all ages and both
sexes.

東京都千代田区丸の内1-9-1
1-9-1, Marunouchi, Chiyoda-ku, Tokyo,
JAPAN
http://www.arincoroll.jp

A, DF: バルニバービ デザインスタジオ
BALNIBARBI DESIGN STUDIO
I: 小西慎一郎　Shinichirou Konishi
CL, SB: バルニバービ　BALNIBARBI

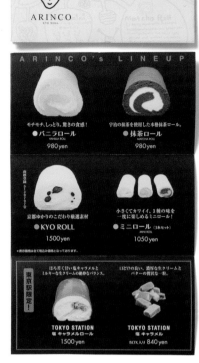

Poster

カフェ／スウィーツ　Cafes / Sweeteries

Doctor Coffee

バルセロナにオープンした特上のコーヒーを提供するカフェ。店名である「ドクター」はコーヒーの専門家や巨匠という意味合いでつけられている。グラフィックにはベリーズ活字を取り入れ、60年代の懐かしいリズム感覚とユーモアを感じさせる店内に仕上げた。また、全体はシリアスで男性的な黒色でまとめ、ところどことコーヒーの茶を効かせた色使いで、落ち着きのある上質感を演出している。

This is a new café in Barcelona, with a selection of top-quality coffees. The name, chosen by the client, suggests specialization or mastership of coffee. We decided to give the graphics a sixties feel like the name, using a Belizio typeface, which transmits rhythm and good humour when upper and lower case are combined.
In order to communicate the high quality of the products, we used a combination of serious, masculine colours, with black backgrounds and small amounts of coffee-coloured brown.

Doctor
Coffee

Passein Sant Joan Basco, 59. 08017
Barcelna, SPAIN
http://www.doctorcoffee.es

CD: Pati Nunez
AD, LD: Kike Segurola
D: Esther Martin de Pozuelo
DF, SB: Pati Nunez Associats
Space Designer: Antoni Arola & Sylvian Carlet
（Estudi Arola）
CL: Lluis Saula

Menu

GÖTGATAN STORIES

親しみやすさや暖かさ、居心地のよさを
全面に出した店内の雰囲気で、若者を
ターゲットとしたカフェ。店名をはじめ、
ツールやパッケージまで統一感がでる
ように心がけ、個性的なカフェ体験の
できる場所となっている。

The challenge was to create a strong and
totally unique cafe experience.
From concept and name, to graphic profile
and packaging. The concept needed to be
warm welcoming, honest and genuine and
targeted to young professionals.

Götgatan 78, 118 30 Stockholm,
SWEDEN

CD: Carin Budholm Svensson
Design Director: Susanna Nygren Barrett
Graphic Designer: Johan Andersson
LD, DF, SB: BVD
CL: Turesgruppen.

ÖTGATAN
ORIES

ON BAKAR VI
SKA RÅVAROR,
TAN ONÖDIGA
RKEN HOS OSS
T UTVALDA

FRÄSCHA
AV KRAVMÄRKTA
ÅVAROR. SPÄNN-
A TILLBEHÖR.
RAT, EXOTISKT
ENSKT.

R EN SMAK-

NJUT AV BIODYNAMISK JUICE
FRÅN SALTÅ KVARN ELLER BÖRJA
DAGEN MED EN NYTTIG SMOOTHIE
FRÅN INNOCENT, DÄR VARJE DRYCK
INNEHÅLLER MINST EN TREDJEDELS
KILO FÄRSKPRESSAD FRUKT.

VÅRT KAFFE ÄR FÄRSKMALET
BRYGGKAFFE I TVÅ VARIANTER
KENYA AA ELLER RÄTTVISEMÄRKT.
ESPRESSOKAFFET ÄR EN BLAND-
NING AV ARABICA-BÖNOR FRÅN
INDIEN OCH GUATEMALA, 100
PROCENT ARABICA.

VÅRA BLOMTEER FRÅN NUMI HAR
EN TUSENÅRIG TRADITION FRÅN

Office Café

CARDINAL CAFÉ

カーディナル・プレイス財団の職員のためのカフェ。キャラクターは、その土地の在来鳥である、カーディナル（猩々紅冠鳥）を意匠化し創られた。また店名は鳥の名からカーディナル・カフェとした。

The cafe is for employees of the cardinal place estate. A character was created inspired by the cardinal bird a title affiliated with the area & therefore lent it's name to cardinal cafe.

CARDINAL CAFÉ

Cardinal Café, Cardinal Place, Victoria, London, UNITED KINGDOM

CD: Jim Sutherland／Gareth Howat
D, LD, I: Adam Giles
Space Designer: Morey Smith
DF, SB: HAT-TRICK DESIGN
CL: Land Securities

Tip Box

ベーカリー＆カフェ

Boulangerie & Café

ヘルシンキ・ベーカリー
Helsinki Bakery

ヘルシンキ在住のAriによるモダンな北欧デザイン。白木や白樺のぬくもりを、ミニマムで洗練された形でデザインしたもの。

Modern Northern European design by Ari, a resident of Helsinki. The warmth of the plain wood and white birch has been designed into minimalist and sophisticated forms.

Helsinki Bakery

兵庫県西宮市高松町14-2
阪急西宮ガーデンズ 2F 202
2F, 14-2-202, Takamatsu-cho,
Nishinomiya-city, Hyogo, JAPAN

D, LD: Arihiro Miyake
CL, SB: ポトマック　POTOMAK Co., ltd.

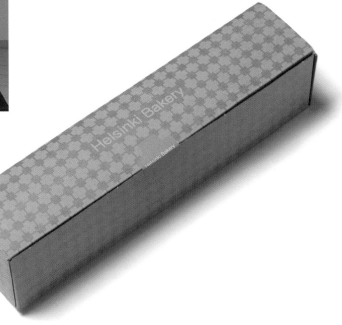

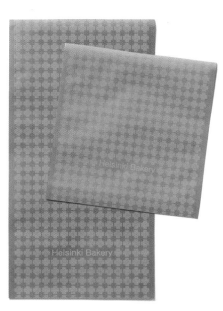

ユーヨーカフェ
YuuYoo CAFE

有機発芽玄米のお粥をはじめ、北海道産中心の有機・減農薬野菜、海産物、乳製品等を使った健康的なオーガニックメニューやスウィーツを楽しめるカフェ。グリーンに基調に展開したツール類が、良質な素材感や北海道のもつ自然を感じさせる。

A café offering a healthy organic menu including rice gruel (okayu) made from organic germinated brown rice. The café uses organic vegetables, seafood and dairy products mainly produced in Hokkaido with reduced use of pesticides. The tools developed in a basic tone of green evoke the idea of high-quality materials and the natural environment of Hokkaido.

東京都港区芝公園1-2-9 ハナイビル1F
1F, 1-2-9, Shiba-Koen, Minato-ku,
Tokyo, JAPAN
http://www.yuuyoo.jp/yuuyoo-cafe

A, Space Designer: 長谷川 演　Hiromu Hasegawa
AF: アトリエテンマ　Atelier-Temma
CD: 寺島賢幸　Masayuki Terashima
AD, D, LD: 藤田直樹　Naoki Fujita
D: 川本真也　Shinya Kawamoto
P: 上村幸将　Yukimasa Uemura
CW: 佐野 亮　Ryo Sano
DF, SB: 寺島デザイン制作室
TERASHIMA DESIGN CO.
CL: ミキコーポレーション　MIKI Corporation

やさしく、しっかり。

毎日を頑張るあなたをいたわりたいから、
YUUYOO CAFEは、
低カロリーで消化吸収がよく、
からだへの負担が少ないお粥にこだわりました。
お米には、有機発芽玄米を厳選。
北海道の神秘の湖
摩周湖のミネラルウォーターで、

有機発芽玄米の、「ピュアなお粥で。

organic
natural
healthy

ORGANIC LIFE BOOK
YuuYoo 手帖

YuuYoo CAFE
HOKKAIDO ORGANIC

はじめまして、
YUUYOOCAFEです。

Vol.01
創刊号

Leaflet

YuuYoo CAFE
HOKKAIDO ORGANIC

MENU

OPEN / CLOSE 8:00～22:00　　MORNING TIME 8:00～10:00
（ラストオーダー21:00）　　LUNCH TIME 11:30～14:30

有機発芽玄米
おかゆ

厳選した有機発芽玄米を北海道の神秘の湖 摩周湖のミネラルウォーターで、
玄米のプチプチ感を残しつつも、やわらかくふっくらと炊き上げました。
日本の最北端 稚内宗谷の自然塩をほの小に利かせた味わいをお楽しみください。

（S:300g M:400g）

プレーン（いめ／つけもの／ねごめこんぶ付け）… S¥450 M¥550
サーモン … S¥560 M¥660
ほたて … S¥600 M¥700
ネバネバきのこ … S¥630 M¥730
根菜 … S¥630 M¥730
ソイビーン＆ベジ … S¥630 M¥730
たらば蟹 … S¥700 M¥800
イタリアン … S¥730 M¥830

トッピング

お好みのトッピングで、あなたにピッタリのおかゆにアレンジ！

お好きな3種類で¥200

半熟たまご … ¥100
梅ぼし … ¥100
揚げ湯葉 … ¥100
青ねぎ … ¥100
ゆで野菜 … ¥100
パルメザンチーズ … ¥100
のり … ¥100
ゴーヤ … ¥100
レタス … ¥100
バジル … ¥100
トマト … ¥100
生ハム … ¥180
ベーコン … ¥180

イートイン専用メニュー
テイクアウト専用メニュー

オーガニック＆ナチュラル
ドリンク

気軽に楽しんでいただきたいからこそ、安心の品質にこだわりました。

じんわりホットミルク … ¥400
すっきりアイスミルク … ¥400
おいしい豆乳ヨーグルト … ¥420
フルーツ畑の有機ジュース
・りんご … ¥500
・オレンジ … ¥500
・フルーツミックス … ¥600
・トマト … ¥600
野菜まるごとジュース … ¥600
野菜たっぷりスープ … ¥500
摩周湖の天然水 500ml … ¥180

有機コーヒーでゆったり
・コーヒー … ¥480
・アイスコーヒー … ¥480
・ホットカフェラテ … ¥580
・アイスカフェラテ … ¥580
・カプチーノ … ¥600
・エスプレッソ … ¥420

有機炭酸でリフレッシュ
・エルダーベリー 330ml … ¥700
・ジンジャーオレンジ 330ml … ¥700
・ライチ 330ml … ¥700

LUNCH TIME お食事時のドリンクは100円OFF（摩周湖の天然水を除く）

オーガニック＆フルーティ
ビール＆ワイン

生ビール 恵比寿 … ¥600
有機ビール … ¥750
有機ワイン 白 グラス ¥580　デカンタ ¥1,800　ボトル ¥2,800
有機ワイン 赤 グラス ¥580　デカンタ ¥1,800　ボトル ¥2,800
有機シャンパン … ¥3,800

ひろがる、
おかゆワールド！

ご注文は
こんなふうに。

おかゆをチョイス

トッピングをプラス

カフェ
Café

ルーフ
Roof

コーヒー、アルコール、アートを気軽に楽しめるカフェ＆バー。1Fは昼間はカフェ、夜間はバー、2Fは食事を楽しみながらギャラリーとしても利用できる。ギャラリーに展示される作品に影響しないよう、全体的にニュートラルな雰囲気に仕上げ、店のロゴもシンプルに力強くデザインした。

A café and bar that offers coffee, alcohol and art. The first floor is a café by day and a bar by night, and the second floor, a restaurant that also serves as a gallery. The overall look is neutral so as not overpower the art works exhibited by the gallery, and the logo has a simple, powerful design.

東京都国分寺市本町 3-12-12
3-12-12, Honmachi, Kokubunji-shi,
Tokyo, JAPAN
http://www.roofhp.com

AD, SB: buffalo-D

2F. gallery

1F. cafe/bar

Roof
cafe. bar. gallery.

🕐 東京都国分寺市本町3-12-12
📞 042-323-7762
✉ roof@sunny.ocn.ne.jp
🕐 open 12:00／close 24:00

Coaster

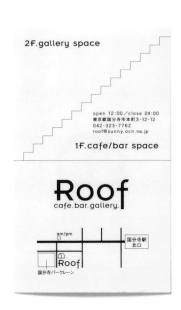

2F. gallery space

open 12:00／close 24:00
東京都国分寺市本町3-12-12
042-323-7762
roof@sunny.ocn.ne.jp

1F. cafe/bar space

Roof
cafe. bar. gallery.

am/pm | 国分寺駅 北口

Roof

国分寺パークレーン

フィヨルド
FJÖRD

目黒通りにて北欧家具を取り扱う
Fusion Interiors が北欧スタイルのカフェ
＆カクテルバーをオープン。北欧を感
じさせるネーミング「フィヨルド」から、
ロゴマーク、DM を開発した。イメージ
カラーをアイスブルーに、店内は暖かみ
のある木でまとめた。

A Scandinavian café and cocktail bar
opened by Fusion Interiors, a Scandinavian furniture store on Meguro-dori. The
logo mark and the DM were developed
from its name of Fjörd that evokes images
of Scandinavia. The store interior was
brought together with warm woods and
an image color of ice blue.

東京都目黒区中町 1-8-12
メグロサンハイム 1F（閉店）
1F, 1-8-12, Nakamachi, Meguro-ku,
Tokyo, JAPAN (Closed)

A: 戸田和寿　Kazuhisa Toda
CD, LD: 川村真司　Masashi Kawamura
AD, LD, SB: 土家啓延　Hironobu Tsuchiya
CL: イグジスト　Exist Limited

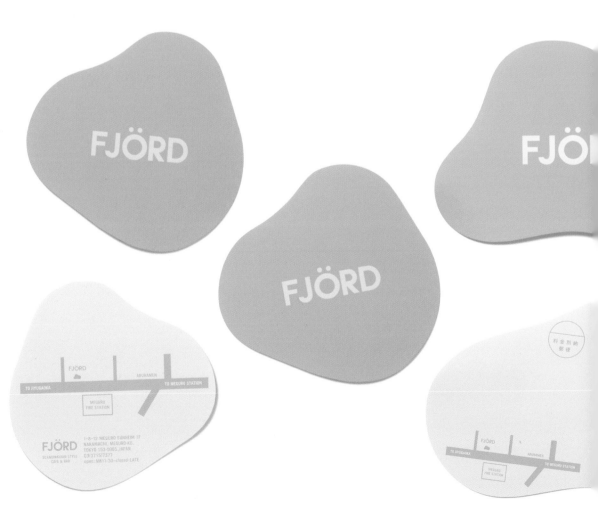

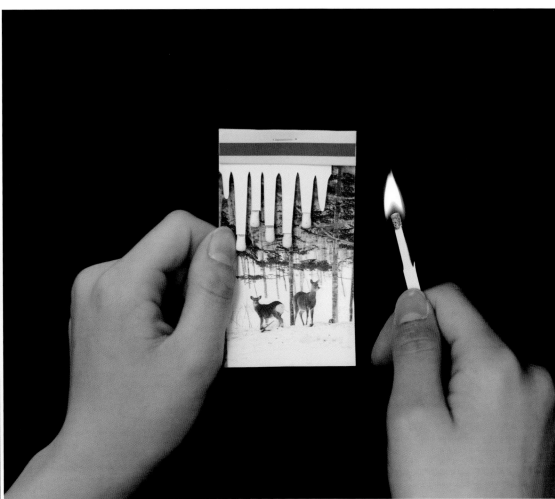

Coaster

喫茶室 豆灯
toutou

喫茶室 豆灯は、古い民家を改装した
キャンドルとコーヒーのお店。温かな雰
囲気の店内では、自家焙煎のコーヒー
とキャンドルのやさしい灯りが時間の
流れを忘れさせてくれる。コーヒーを表
す「豆」とキャンドルを表す「灯」の文字
をレトロなトーンでマーク化し、グラ
フィックを展開。

Toutou candle and coffee shop located
inside a renovated old private home. In
the warm ambience of the shop, the
coffee made with beans that are roasted
in house and the gentle light of the
candles make time stand still for a while.
The graphics were developed by turning
the Japanese characters for "bean"
representing coffee and for "light" representing candles into retro-style marks.

北海道網走郡美幌町仲町2-80-1
2-80-1, Nakamachi, Bihoro-cho,
Abashiri-gun, Hokkaido, JAPAN

AD, D, LD: 藤田直樹　Naoki Fujita
I: 杉田 遥　Haruka Sugita
DF: ハモニカビル　harmonica bldg.
DF, SB: 寺島デザイン制作室　TERASHIMA
DESIGN CO.
CL: 喫茶室 豆灯　toutou

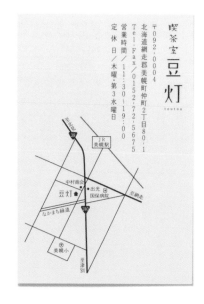

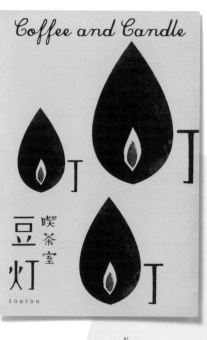

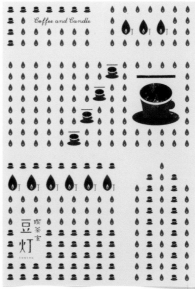
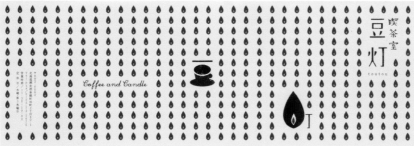
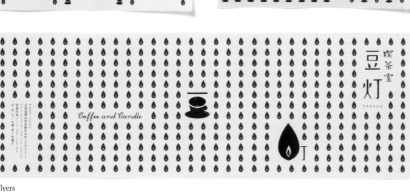

Flyers

カフェ

Café

カフェウミエ
cafe umie

元々50年前に建てられた穀物倉庫を、デザインオフィスとして使用する予定だったが、カフェとしてスタート。海のすぐそばにある錆びたトタンの建物で、ゆったりと過ごしてもらいたくて、「A little bit cozier life-style（ほんのちょっとの心地いい暮らし）」をコンセプトに、ライブ、ブックフェア、ギャラリーなどを展開している。

The plan was to use the granary that had been originally built 50 years ago as a design office, but instead a café was opened. Live gigs, book fairs and a gallery among other things have been developed upon the concept of "a little bit cozier life-style" where visitors are encouraged to spend a relaxing time in the rusty tin building on the edge of the sea.

umie

香川県高松市北浜町3-2（北浜 alley-h）
Kitahama alley-h, 3-2 Kitahama-cho,
Takamatsu-City, Kagawa, JAPAN
http://www.umie.info

AD, P: 柳沢高文　Takafumi Yanagisawa
D: 住野真紀子　Makiko Sumino／豊田恭子
Kyoko Toyota
PL, CW: 川井知子　Tomoko Kawai
DF, SB: ドリームネットワークアクティビティ
Dream Network Activity

DM

Member's Card

エーキューナナイチ
カフェ
A971 CAFE

"Think Global, Respect Local" というコンセプトをそのままに、「食する場」を中心に「東京の今」を感じる音楽、アート、デザイン等のコンテンツを感じられる場（＝カフェ）としてシンガポールにオープン。東京にある本店のデザインを軸に、両都市の持つパワーやカルチャーを表現している。

The concept is Think Global, Respect Local. The focus of the café that has opened in Singapore is on dining, but here you can also experience the music, art and design of the "now" of Tokyo. Centered around the design of the parent restaurant in Tokyo, the restaurant encapsulates the power and the culture of both cities.

30 Marchant Road #01-04, Riverside Point, SINGAPORE 058282
http://www.a971.com

A: 當間一弘　Kazuhiro Toma／加藤百合子
Yuriko Kato
AF, DF, CL, SB: カフェ・カンパニー
CAFE COMPANY INC.
CD: 楠本修二郎　Shujiro Kusumoto
AD: 飯島広昭　Hiroaki Iijima
D: 椿原大平　Taihei Tsubakihara／百瀬庸子
Yoko Momose
P: 谷口 京　Kei Taniguchi
Product Designer: 濱名 剛　Takeshi Hamana

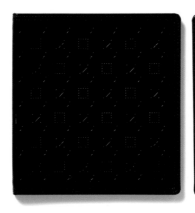

Flyer

Delis
/
Light fare

ポワン エ リーニュ
POINT ET LIGNE

ショップの区間のほぼ中央に、コンベクションオーブンをシンボリックに設置。パンを製造する側とパンを購入する側とをボーダレスにライブ感を演出。奥に鮮やかなピンク色の壁面を配し、バールへの誘導としている。新丸ビルという立地もあり、ファッションブランドのようなパン屋さんをイメージした。ピンクをテーマカラーにして、よい香りのするパンのブランド化をグラフィックで表現している。

A convection oven was symbolically installed in the center of a section of the shop, with the idea of creating a "live" atmosphere and removing the boundary between the bakers of the bread and the customers. A bright pink wall leading to the bar was placed at the back. The image is "a bakery as a fashion brand," which fits in with its location inside the Shinmaru Building. With pink as the theme color, graphics were used to create a brand from the delicious aromas of fresh bread.

POINT ET LIGNE

東京都千代田区丸の内1-5-1
新丸の内ビルB1
B1, 1-5-1, Marunouchi, Chiyoda-ku,
Tokyo, JAPAN
http://www.point-et-ligne.com

A: 斉藤真司（タイプ・ワン） Shinji Saito
（TYPE-ONE）
AD, LD: 若山嘉代子 Kayoko Wakayama
D: 黒田麻美 Mami Kuroda
DF: レスパース L'espace
SB: ケイアンドエイ K & A

POINT ET LIGNE

Hors-d'oeuvre 前菜

1. 豚肩ロースのブレゼ エシャロット添え ￥420
 〜口サイズのオードブル とりあえずどうぞ

2. ピリ辛ミックスオリーブ ￥400
 6種類のスパイスでピリッと…お酒がススミます

3. 鴨パテ ￥650
 パテに近いフランス伝統的な鴨肉で…パンがつまめ

4. 砂肝とモッツァレラチーズのサラダ仕立て ￥750
 砂肝のコンフィをモッツァレラチーズの上に重ねるよ…ア

5. 牡蠣のオイル漬け ￥800
 牡蠣、柿、柿のサラダ仕立て ワインに合います

6. スモークサーモン ￥850
 〜スモークラウドで自時燻製品

Staub 無別オーブンメニュー

7. ジャガイモとミートソースのグラタン ￥650
 熱い状態には熱々をどうぞ

8.10 種類の野菜のミネストローネ ￥650
 辛口ケマ混ぜの素材々を召し上がってください

9. 海老とさきこの香草パン粉焼き ￥700
 海老とジュノバゼリースのこの香草をどうぞ

10. 豚肉とインカのめざめの白ワイン煮込み ￥750
 ゴロっと大きめの豚肉とインカのめざめをじっくり煮込みまし

Plats メイン

11. 鴨モモ肉のコンフィ ￥1,100
 骨付鴨のモモはボリュームたっぷり

12. 帆立貝のポワレ ￥1,200
 大きい帆立をラタトイユと一緒にお召し上がりください

13. スモークサーモンのミキュイ ￥1,200
 皮の旨みパリッと焼き上げた絶品のスモークサーモン

Extras サイドオーダー

14. パンの盛合わせ ￥300
 追加オーダーは100yen

15. 自家製合わせバター ￥150
 サービスにお重ねください

16. 季節のコンフィチュール ￥150
 サービスにお重ねください

Desserts デザート

17. パンプディング ￥550
 グリーンレーズンとカカオのパンに生姜を利かせた大人のプディング

18. クレームブリュレ ￥600
 フランスディジョン産スパイス使用パンの濃厚クレームブリュレ

19. ティラミス ￥650
 マスカルポーネとエスプレッソゼリーのマリアージュをお楽しみください

Vins ワイン

Vin Moussseux スパークリングワイン

クレマン ダルザス ブリュット
Crémant d'Alsace Brut N.V. / A.O.C.
クリーミィな泡立ち、爽やかでコクがあるアルザスらしい味わいの

Glass ￥800 / Bottle ￥4,800

Vin Blanc 白ワイン

シャトー ド ヴィオニエ
Chateau de Rieux Viognier 2006
黄すもぎ等の香り、穏かな酸のバランスが良い辛口白ワインです

Glass ￥600 / Bottle ￥3,800

シャルドネ
Chardonnay 2005 (Newton Johnson)
程よい酸にバターのようなニュアンス、厚い余韻を残します

Glass ￥700 / Bottle ￥4,400

Vin Rouge 赤ワイン

トリエンヌ オーレリアン ルージュ 2005
Triennes Les Aurliens 2005
豊かな果実味、力強さと樽熟成のバランスがよい南仏赤ワイン

Glass ￥650 / Bottle ￥4,000

トリンケロ バルベラ ダスティ スペリオーレ 2001
Trinchero Barbera d'Asti Superiore 2001
滋味い果実味、しっかりとしたボディと果実味の自然派ワインです

Glass ￥800 / Bottle ￥4,600

※上記以外に、ボトルワインも多数ご用意しております。サービスにお尋ねください。

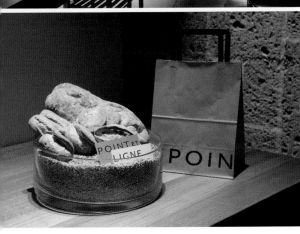

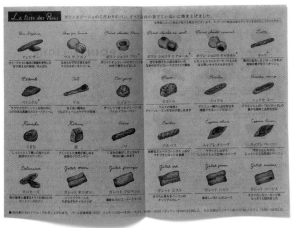

ブーランジュリー

Boulangerie

デュヌ・ラルテ
d'une rareté

店名の「類いにも稀なる」という意味どおり、類稀なパン屋でありたい、東京の生活者である自分自身が気持ちよく食べられるパンを作りたい‥‥。そして「パンも料理そのもの」という考えで、今までの常識を排除したところから生まれたおしゃれなベーカリー専門店。

As the name which translates as "There's almost nothing else like it" suggests, the objective was to create an almost one-of-a-kind bakery that produces delicious bread products for Tokyo dwellers. A stylish specialty bakery store that deviates from conventional wisdom, with the idea that bread is also "cuisine."

東京都渋谷区神宮前 5-10-1
ジャイル B1F
B1F, 5-10-1, Jingumae, Shibuya-ku,
Tokyo, JAPAN
http://www.dune-rarete.com

A: 斉藤真司（タイプ・ワン）　Shinji Saito
（TYPE-ONE）
CL, SB: コモンリード　Common Lead

ビー　ブーランジェ
ピシエ

be-boulangépicier

「お持ち帰りできるレストランの味」を
コンセプトに、アラン・デュカスがプロ
デュースするショップ。パンやオリーヴ
オイルなど、商品の特長を表した色を
ベースにロゴをシンプルにデザインし
たパッケージや心地よさを感じさせる
店舗デザインは、手づくりの伝統とフレ
ンチオーセンティック＆モダニティとい
うbeの世界を表現。

A shop produced by Alain Ducasse based
on the concept of "the flavors of the
restaurant for you to take home." The
packaging, with its simple design for the
logo, based on colors that showcase the
products, such as bread and olive oil, and
the comfortable design of the store
interior, create the world of "be" from the
tradition of the home-made and French
authenticity and modernity.

東京都新宿区新宿 3-14-1
伊勢丹新宿店 B1
B1F ISetan Shinjuku, 3-14-1 Shinjuku,
Shinjuku-ku, Tokyo, JAPAN

CL, SB: アンデルセン be事業部
ANDERSEN Co., Ltd. be Division

はちみつ専門店 ラベイユ 荻窪本店

L'abeille

南仏のメゾンをイメージした自然の温もりを感じさせる店内に、はちみつの美しさを生かしたシンプルなデザインを展開。日々の生活を楽しむための"はちみつのある暮らし"を提案している。

A simple design utilizing the beauty of honey was developed for the shop that exudes the natural warmth of the south of France. The shop offers "a lifestyle that incorporates honey" for the enjoyment of everyday life.

東京都杉並区天沼3-6-23
3-6-23 Amanuma, Suginami-ku, Tokyo,
JAPAN
http://www.labeille.jp

A: 岡本勝政　Katsumasa Okamoto
D: 濱本絵里　Eri Hamamoto
SB: 田頭養蜂場　Tagashira Yohojou Co., ltd.

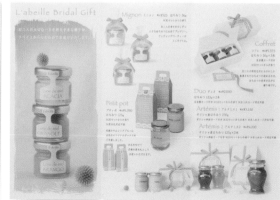

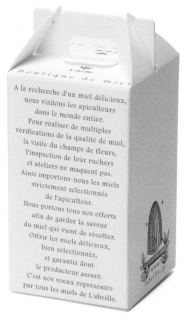

NEW ZEALAND

White clover comb honey

A la recherche d'un miel délicieux,
nous visitons les apiculteurs
dans le monde entier.
Pour réaliser de multiples
vérifications de la qualité de miel,
la visite du champs de fleurs,
l'inspection de leur ruchers
et ateliers ne maquent pas.
Ainsi importons-nous les miels
strictement selectionnés
de l'apiculteur.
Nous portons tous nos efforts
afin de garder la saveur
du miel qui vient de récolter.
Offrir les miels délicieux,
bien selectionnés,
et garantis dont
le producteur assuré.
C'est nos voeux représentés
par tous les miels de L'abeille.

SPÉCIALITÉS
Bonbons au miel
L'abeille

SPÉCIALITÉS
Confiture au miel
L'abeille

SPÉCIALITÉS
Confiture au miel
L'abeille

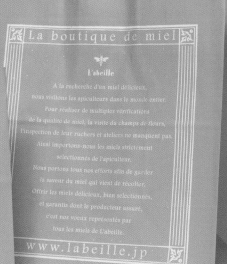

La boutique de miel
L'abeille
www.labeille.jp

ジュノエスクベーグル
JUNOESQUE BAGEL

ジュノエスクのベーグルは合成着色料、合成保存料等を一切使用していない。美味しくて体にやさしいベーグルは卵やバターも使用しておらず、アトピーのお子さんや赤ちゃんの歯固めにも適している。健康でナチュラルなライフスタイルを送るこれからの家族に心地よく信頼されるブランドイメージを描いたデザイン。

Bagels that contain no artificial colors or preservatives nor any butter or eggs are also good for teething infants or babies who have allergies. The design depicts a brand image readily trusted by families of the future who lead a healthy, natural lifestyle.

JUNOESQUE BAGEL

東京都大田区鵜の木3-13-13
3-13-13, Unoki, Ota-ku, Tokyo, JAPAN
http://www.junoesque.jp

AD, P: 柳沢高文　Takafumi Yanagisawa
D: 住野真紀子　Makiko Sumino／豊田恭子
Kyoko Toyota
CW, Planner: 川井知子　Tomoko Kawai
DF, SB: ドリームネットワークアクティビティ
Dream Network Activity
CL: ジュノエスクベーグル
JUNOESQUE BAGEL

ホットドッグショップ

Hotdog Shop

エキタマ
ekitama

駅の構内に新しいたまごを生み出し、そのたまごから「『新しいモノ』『新しいコト』が生まれ出る」をコンセプトとし、エキナカであらゆる人が集い、コミュニケーションをとるきっかけになるよう、ツールに遊び心を盛り込んだ。機能優先の直線的な駅において、有機的な丸いフォルムの外観はやわらかな存在感を与えている。エ、キ、タ、マのそれぞれの文字を重ねて、アンテナを立てたものがロゴになっているが、あらゆる人が集い、重なり、エキタマで新しいことが発信、受信できコミュニケーションがとれるようにとの想いが詰まっている。

With the concept of "new things" emerging from the "new egg" in the station precinct, a sense of fun was incorporated into the tools to get different kinds of people to gather inside the station and to create an opportunity for communication. In a station constructed from straight lines where functionality is a priority, the organic round form was a gentle presence. The logo was produced from the characters e, ki, ta and ma stacked one on top of the other with a raised antenna, but the idea of it was a place where different kinds of people gather together at the same time and can transmit and receive news at the ekitama as a means of communication.

東京都港区芝5-33-36 JR田町駅構内
JR Tamachi Station, 5-33-36, Shiba,
Minato-ku, Tokyo, JAPAN
http://www.ecute.jp/ekitama/

CD: 服部滋樹
Hattori Shigeki (graf:decrative mode no.3)
A: 大薗貴生
Takao Ozono (graf:decrative mode no.3)
LD: 横山道雄
Michio Yokoyama (graf:decrative mode no.3)
CL, SB: JR東日本ステーションリテイリング
JR East Station Retailing Co., Ltd.

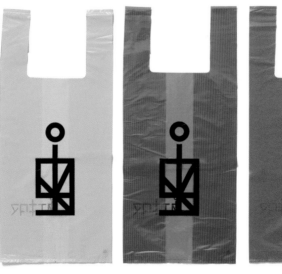

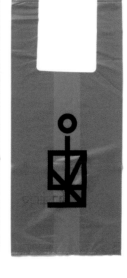

スムーチ 山王パークタワー店
smooch Sanno Park Tower Shop

「ナチュラルエナジーカフェ」をコンセプトに、体に嬉しいデリシャス＆ヘルシーなスナック、上質なフルーツを使った本格スムージー専門店。店内は「芝生の上に転がりながら青空を見上げよう」というメッセージを込めて白、緑、そしてピンクのポップな色を使用。無機質なオフィスビルの一角を遊び心で彩る都会のオアシスを目指した。

A specialty genuine smoothie store that uses delicious and healthy snacks and top-quality fruits, with a "natural energy café" concept. The store interior uses the pop colors of white, green and pink to encapsulate the idea of "looking up at a blue sky while stretched out on a lawn." The objective was to make a corner of an inorganic office building into an urban oasis awash with fun colors.

デリ／軽食 Delis / Light fare

東京都千代田区永田町2-11-1
山王パークタワー1F
1F, 2-11-1, Nagata-cho, Chiyoda-ku,
Tokyo, JAPAN
http://www.smooch.co.jp

Shop Designer: アッタ　ATTACo., Ltd.
Equipment Designer:
ディッシモ一級建築士事務所　decimo
SB: スムーチジャパン　Smooch Japan

Press Release

mangiare

サンドイッチ・ランチと同価格帯で、本物のイタリア料理を販売する店。半透明の黄色の帯が、ファサードの下部に施され、黄色いアイデンティティを強調し、同時に窓際のスツールに座る客に対して適度のスクリーンを提供。オークのパネルに黄色、淡いグレー、濃いグレーが挿入された長く特徴ある無規則で3次元的にリズミカルな壁は、メニューボードを組み入れて、空間のカウンター側へ、視覚焦点をつくる。グラフィックと写真は、店内の「イタリアン・ホーム・クッキング」のアイデアを伝えるため、キッチン近くの壁全体を華やかに、並んでいる客によく見えるようデザインされた。

Mangiare sells authentic, hot Italian food at a price that compares with a sandwich lunch. A semi-opaque yellow band was added to the to lower section of the façade to reinforce the "yellow identity" as well as provide a modesty screen for customers sitting on stools at the window. A long wall of oak slats with inset yellow, light and dark grey panels formed a "random" rhythmic three-dimensional visual focus to the servery side of the space incorporating the signage for the menu boards. Graphics and photography were designed to take up an entire wall adjacent to the kitchen and in full view of queuing customers in order to get across the idea of 'Italian home cooking' on the premises.

デリ／軽食　Delis / Light fare

157-158 London Wall, City of London,
EC2M 5QQ , UNITED KINGDOM
http://www.mangiare.co.uk

AD, SB: Rashna Mody Clark
Architect／Interiors: Jonathan Clark Architects
CL: Mangiare

NUSA KITCHEN

アジアにインスパイアを受けてオープ
ンした、家族経営によるスープ専門店
の第2号店。ナチュラルで上質、そして
新鮮な素材を、手軽におしゃれに楽し
んでもらうという狙いからシンプルでキ
ャッチーなデザインを心がけ、1号店よ
りも人気を博している。

The second of a family-run Asian-inspired
specialty soup store. The second store is
enjoying even more popularity than the
first, with a simple, catchy design in
accordance with the concept of casual yet
stylish enjoyment of high-quality, fresh
natural ingredients.

Adams Court, London, UNITED
KINGDOM
http://www.nusakitchen.com

D, LD: Tom Collins
P: Matt Stuart
DF, SB: Third Person
CL: Nusa Kitchen

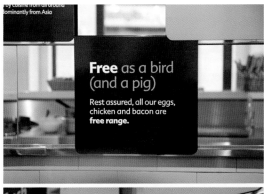

Bocí

カタロニア語で「ほんの一部分」を意味
する Boci という名のパティスリー＆デ
リ。ロゴは丸い形をモチーフに網目状の
ドットで表現し、料理やその材料が写っ
たフルカラーやモノクロの写真が飾ら
れている。パッケージにはロゴと同様に
丸い形をあしらった。

A patisserie and delicatessen selling
ready-cooked meals, it was called Mos
until recently. They chose Bocí, which
means "a little piece" in Catalan. We
started this time from a circle as the
structure for the logo and also used
halftone dots for the images: we halftoned
photos of ingredients and food, sometimes
in full colour and others in just one colour.
The logo is used with a circle round it
found packaging and without the circle in
items such as cards and the paper bag.

 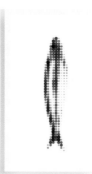  

Via Augusta, 112. 08006 Barcelona,
SPAIN
http://www.boci.cat

CD, AD: Pati Nunez
D, AD, LD: Kike Segurola
DF: Pati Nunez Associats
Space Designer: Antoni Arola（Estudi Arola）
CL: Joaquim Llobera

Gourmet Market

BUTTERFIELD MARKET

1915年開店以来、品質、サービスともに上級で知られる家族経営の食糧雑貨店。店舗とその周辺、そしてNYの人々の気品と折衷主義を視覚言語と様式により具現化し、"Lex"、"between 77th & 78th"、"NYC"などの語の使用で、顧客との文化的、地理的結びつきを表現。グラフィックスは上品に納まりすぎないよう特大の画像と、モダン・ミントとなすび色を使用。人目を引くショッパーなどでブランドの存在感を示した。

A family-owned grocery famous for its superior quality and customer service since its establishment on New York's Upper East Side in 1915. The visual language and style embody the elegance and eclecticism of the market, the neighborhood, and New Yorkers: using the terms "Lex", "between 77th & 78th" and "NYC" communicates the market's cultural and geographic connection with its customers. Referencing the market's history was important, as was the way the historical references were interpreted. As opposed to politely sitting in their space, the graphics are super-sized in all applications, and utilize a modern mint and eggplant palette. The highly recognizable delivery van, box and shopping bag extend the brand presence beyond the marketplace onto the streets of the city.

1114 Lexington Avenue
New York, NY 10021, U.S.A
http://www.butterfieldmarket.com

CD: Matteo Bologna
AD, D: Christine Celic Strohl
D: Lauren Sheldon
DF, SB: Mucca Design Corp.
CL: Butterfield Market

Roadside Diner

LITTLE CHEF Popham

ミシュランの星を持つシェフ、ヘストン・ブルーメンソールとアブ・ロジャーズ・デザインの新しい、未来へ向けた、ポファムのリトル・シェフは、新鮮な料理、優れたサービス、積極性において現代21世紀ロンドンの最高級を表した、多様に官能的なオアシスそして隠れ家。

Michelin star chef Heston Blumenthal and Ab Rogers Design's new future-facing Little Chef in Popham is a multi-sensual oasis, an escape that reflects the best of modern 21st century Britain: fresh food, good service, and positive attitude.

Popham(A303West), Micheldever,
Hampshire, S021 3SP,
UNITED KINGDOM
http://www.littlechef.co.uk

CD, AD: Ab Rogers
D: YeonjuYang／Yosuke Watanabe
P: Little Chef／Ab Rogers Design／Praline
LD: Graphic Design Studio "Praline"（Shop Tool）
DF, SB: Ab Rogers Design／Praline
Space Design: Ab Rogers Design
Interactive Design: Dominic Robson
（Robson & Jones）
CL: Little Chef

Pin Badges

バルバラ・ポータブル
BARBARA PORTABLE

店舗イメージは、「貝殻(SHELL)」、「工場(FACTORY)」、そして「白(WHITE)」。「貝殻(SHELL)」は、曲線を帯びた幾何学的な貝殻、鎧の構造、甲殻類のデザイン、単純なパーツをくり返すことによってできる機能美をイメージしている。「工場(FACTORY)」は、機能美を見せること。料理を作る機械をわざと見せるパフォーマンスなど。「白(WHITE.)」は、クリーン・シンプル・ミニマム。貝殻、工場のイメージともリンクしている。

The store's images are "shell," "factory" and "white." Shell represents a functional beauty that can be achieved by repetitions of curved geometric shells, the structure of armor, the design of crustacea and simple components. Factory demonstrates a functional beauty, a performance that intentionally displays the machinery that does the cooking. White is clean, simple and minimal. Images of shell and factory are also linked.

東京都新宿区新宿3-38-2 ルミネ2 1F
1F, 3-38-2, Shinjuku, Shinjuku-ku, Tokyo, JAPAN
http://www.b-barbara.com

LD, D: ハヤシジュンジロウ　Junjiro Hayashi
CL, SB: ポトマック　POTOMAK Co., ltd.

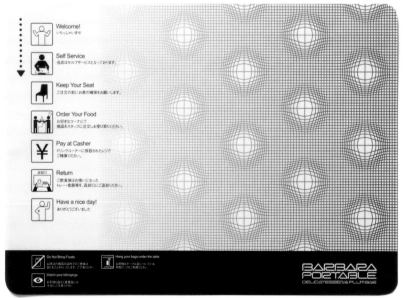

Paper Plate Mat

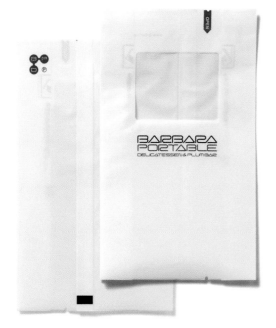

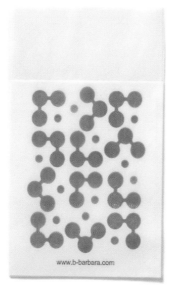

Contemporary Mexican Taqueria

GUZMAN Y GOMEZ

オーストラリアへ進出した、Taqueria
チェーン店による、本格的なメキシカン
フードの飲食店。

Guzman Y Gomez is a new-to-world
chain of taqueria stores specialising in
bringing authentic Mexican cuisine to the
Australian public.

GUZMAN Y GOMEZ HEAD OFFICE LEVEL 1 209 GLENMORE RD.
PADDINGTON, NSW 2021 T: (02) 9380 9779 F: (02) 9380 9778
M: 0416 368 792 E: steven@guzmanygomez.com
www.guzmanygomez.com

STEVEN MARKS
MANAGING DIRECTOR

Auténtico, Mexicano, Delicioso

175 King Street, Newtown, NSW, 2042
AUSTRALIA
http://www.guzmanygomez.com

A, Space Designer: Brad Ward
CD, AD, LD: Tony Ibbotson
D: Tony Ibbotson／Andi Yanto
DF, P, Space Designer, SB: The Creative Method
CL: Guzman Y Gomez Mexican Taqueria

VILA VINITECA

ワイン専門店として出発した店が、美味
しいワインを楽しめるレストランをオー
プン。独自のワインも生産しており、テ
イスティングスクールを運営、また新し
いワイナリーをも成功させている。たく
さんのワイングラスや飲料の写真を撮
り、いろいろな色で描き、「このお店に
は数多くのワインのコレクションとワイ
ンの味が楽しめる」という唯一のコンセ
プトを表現している。

Beginning as a wine shop, it soon became
a supplier to the best restaurants in the
country. Vila Viniteca also produces its
own wines, organizes wine-tasting courses
and has forged the success of new wineries.
Then we took photos of glasses of wine
and other drinks to illustrate the hundreds
of colours and range of tastes to be found
in a wine shop, with bird's-eye viewpoints,
not showing the glass or the bottle, to
reinforce the single concept of "collection
of tastes".

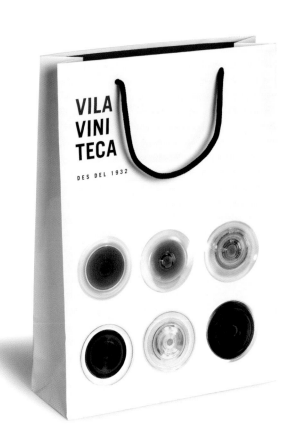

VILA VINI TECA

DES DEL 1932

Agullers, 7. 08003 Barcelona, SPAIN
http://www.vilaviniteca.es

CD, AD, LD,P: Pati Nunez
D: Kike Segurola
DF, SB: Pati Nunez Associats
CL: Quim Vila

Thai Delicatessen

マンゴツリーデリ

mango tree deli

伝統的タイ料理をカジュアルに提供するマンゴツリーの世界を、いつでも自由に楽しんでもらいたい、という目的で作られた初のテイクアウト専門店。見栄えも大事にするレストランの方針を受け継いで、カラフルなボウルやボックスで、見た目にも楽しいテイクアウトのパッケージを使用している。

The first takeaway outlet for Mango Tree, a restaurant business based in Bangkok offering traditional Thai cuisine at your convenience. The look incorporates the restaurant's valued ethos, and the colorful bowls and boxes used to pack the food make for a fun takeaway experience.

mango tree deli
Authentic Thai Cuisine

東京都千代田区丸の内1-9-1
JR東日本東京駅構内B1F
GranSta B1F, 1-9-1 Marunouchi,
Chiyoda-ku, Tokyo, JAPAN
http://www.restaurant-mrs.com/shoplist/
mangotreedeli.html

CL, SB: M・R・S

Restaurants / Bars

kitchen.

ベトナムの元気のよさ、明るさ、楽しさ、おいしさ、奥の深さを感じられるベトナム料理店。既成概念の中にあるイメージとは違ったkitchen.というお店のフィルターを通したイメージで表現したいと考えた。

A Vietnamese restaurant where you can experience the vitality, fun and delicious flavors of Vietnam. The idea was to express an image of a kitchen different from existing ideas of a kitchen, through the filter of the restaurant.

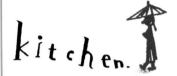

東京都港区西麻布4-4-12
ニュー西麻布ビル2F
2F, 4-4-12, Nishi-Azabu, Minato-ku,
Tokyo, JAPAN
http://www.fc-arr.com/kitchen/

CD, AD, D, LD: 田中竜介　Ryusuke Tanaka
DF, SB: ドラフト　DRAFT Co., Ltd.

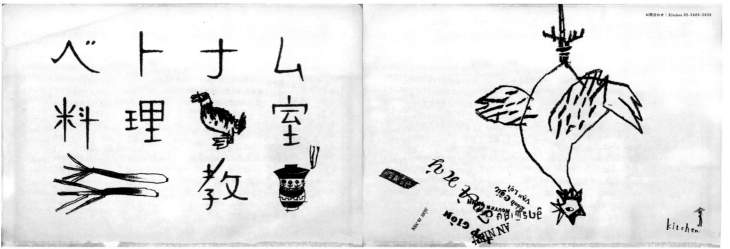

Posters

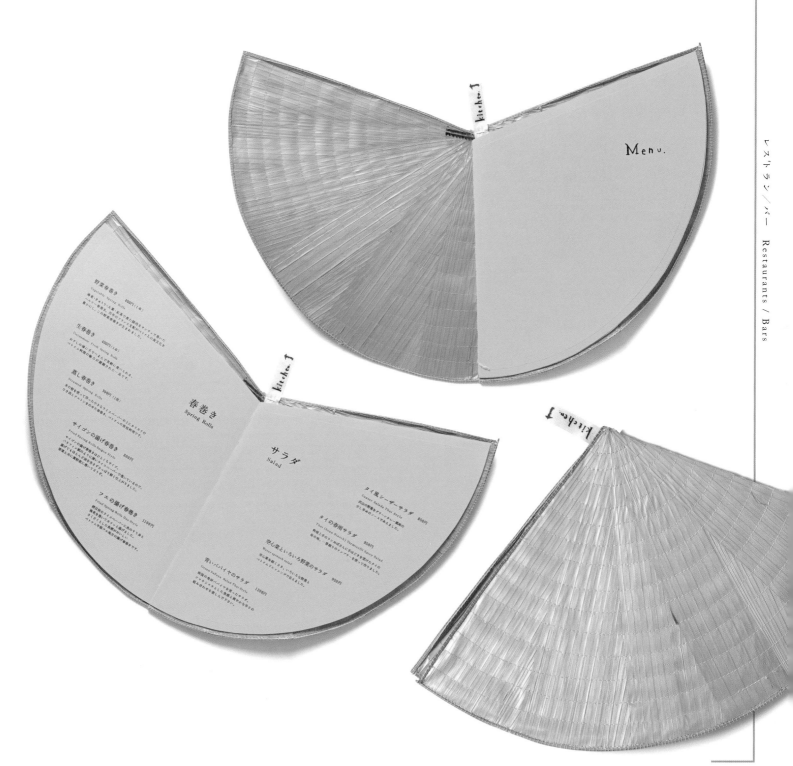

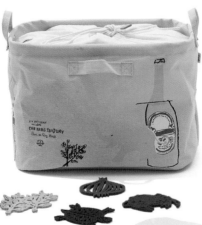

おでん料理店

Oden Restaurant

おでん三六九
Oden Miroku

「三六九」という店名から、三角形、六角形、九角形をモチーフにデザインした。まるでおでんを抽象化した形であり、「和モダン」を感じるたたずまいをめざした。「新おでん屋さん」である。

From the restaurant's name, 369, triangles, hexagons and nonagons became the motif. The objective was a shape based on a completely abstracted oden and a look that suggested "Japanese modern." A new style for the traditional oden restaurant.

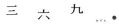

東京都杉並区高円寺南3-45-11
3-45-11, Koenji-minami, Suginami-ku, Tokyo, JAPAN

A, Space Designer: 中島雄一郎
Yuichiro Nakajima
CD, AD, D, LD: 小杉幸一　Koichi Kosugi
P: 岡 祐介　Yusuke Oka
CL: 三六九　Miroku
SB: 博報堂　HAKUHODO Inc.

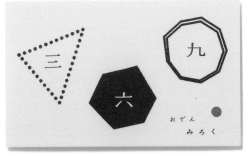

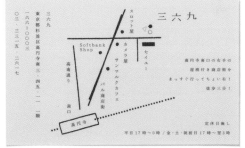

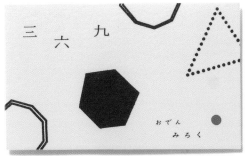

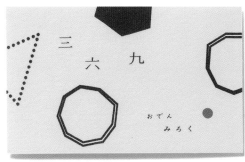

オリヂナルジョーズ
Original Joe's

海沿いに位置する爽やかなイタリアンレストラン。店内で目にするさまざまなツール類に親しみやすく可愛らしいイラストをほどこすことで、幅広く受け入れやすい店づくりを目指した。

A fresh Italian restaurant located on the seashore. The objective was to create a spacious and accessible restaurant using friendly, cute illustrations for the various tools that can be spotted throughout the restaurant.

神奈川県鎌倉市由比ガ浜1-10-10
1-10-10, Yuigahama, Kamakura-city,
Kanagawa, JAPAN

AD, D: 福田 航　Ko Fukuda
D, I: 大間 猛　Takeshi Ohma
P: 黒澤康成　Yasunari Kurosawa
CL: オリヂナルジョーズ　Original Joe's
SB: マーキング・デザイン・カンパニー
marking design company

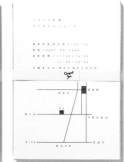

Coasters

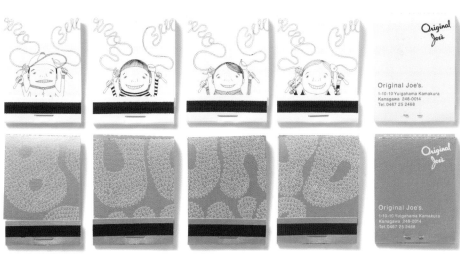

Original Joe's.
1-10-10 Yuigahama Kamakura
Kanagawa 248-0014
Tel: 0467 25 2468

Original Joe's.
1-10-10 Yuigahama Kamakura
Kanagawa 248-0014
Tel: 0467 25 2468

Menu

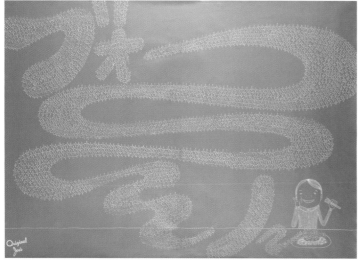

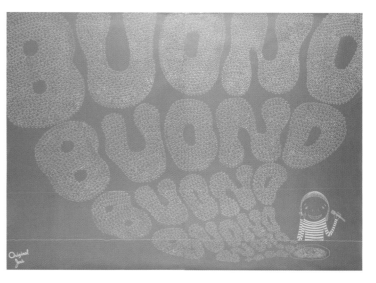

Posters

Basta così!

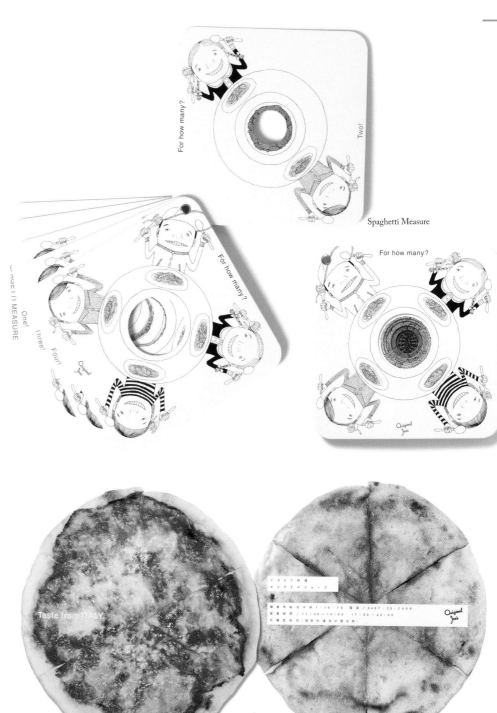

Spaghetti Measure

Shop Card

Taste from ITALY.

Taste from ITALY.

Posters

Dinning Bar

アジト ワンダー ダイニング
AJITO WONDER DINING

渋谷のおいしいアジトとして、ひっそりと佇むダイニングバー。室内は部屋のようにくつろげる。ロゴは、小さい時にアジト（基地）などを作る際によく使った「枝」や「丸太」をモチーフに、いろいろなものに展開できるイメージをデザインした。

A dining bar that stands quietly as a delicious hiding place in Shibuya. You can relax here as if it were your own home. The logo has a motif of the branches and logs we used as children to build hiding places, and the images designed can be developed into a diversity of things.

東京都渋谷区道玄坂1-18-4
和田ビル2F
2F, 1-18-4 Dogenzaka, Shibuya-ku,
Tokyo, JAPAN
http://www.ajito.in/

A: 常岡晋太郎　Shintaro Tsuneoka
CD, AD, D, LD: 小杉幸一　Koichi Kosugi
CL: アジト　ajito
SB: 博報堂　HAKUHODO Inc.

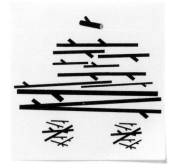

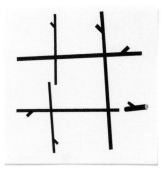

Coasters

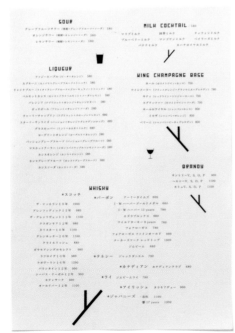

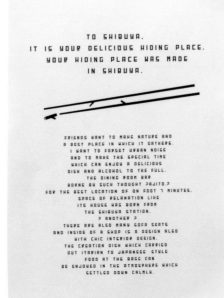

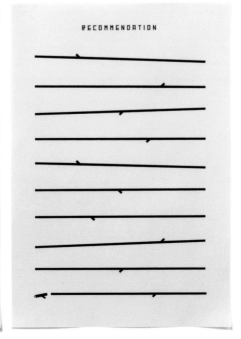

豚肉料理専門店

Pork Restaurant

ぶた家
BUTAYA

『ぶた家』というユニークな名前のイメージを、デザインしすぎて壊さないようにと考えた。香港の裏通りで地元の人から親しまれているお店をイメージし、ずっと前からあったような雰囲気を意識した。

The idea was not to over-design and thereby ruin the image of the uniquely named Buta-ya (Pig pen). The focus instead was on the atmosphere of a backstreet joint in Hong Kong known and loved by locals, with the feel that its been around for ages.

東京都渋谷区恵比寿西1-4-11
1-4-11, Ebisun-nishi, Shibuya-ku, Tokyo, JAPAN
http://www.butaya.co.jp

AD: 永井裕明　Hiroaki Nagai
D: 高橋かおる　Kaoru Takahashi
DF, SB: エヌ・ジー　N.G.INC.,

Coaster

Stickers

レストラン／バー　Restaurants / Bars

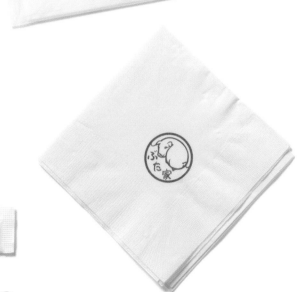

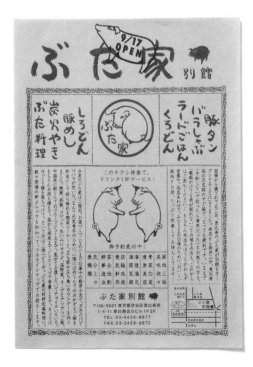

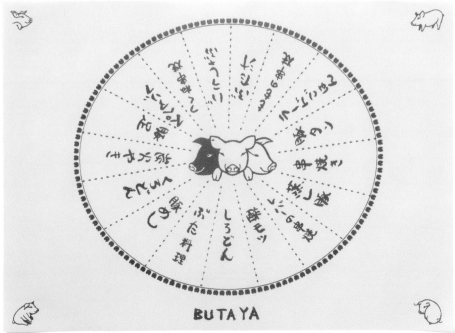

Paper Plate Mat

ニホンバシイチノイチノイチ
Nihonbashi ichi no ichi no ichi

街道の起点として、また、江戸の中心と
して栄えた東京・日本橋。日本の伝統と
文化が息づく街にふさわしい新しい名
所として、全国から厳選した食材を用い
た「日本の食」を楽しめる和食レストラ
ンである。

Nihonbashi in Tokyo, a place that
prospered as the starting point of the
highway and as the center of the Edo
world. A Japanese restaurant for
enjoyment of the "cuisine of Japan" for
which carefully selected ingredients from
around Japan have been used. A new
place of note that befits an area filled with
Japanese tradition and culture.

Sticker

Novelty

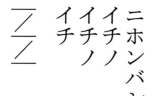

ニホンバシ
イチノ
イチノ
イチ

Nihonbashi 1-1-1

東京都中央区日本橋 1-1-1
国分ビルディング 1F
1F, 1-1-1, Nihonbashi, Chuo-ku, Tokyo,
JAPAN
http://www.zetton.co.jp

A: 中村拓志　Hiroshi Nakamura
AF: NAP建築設計事務所
NAP ARCHITECTS CO., LTD.
CD: 梶田知嗣　Tomotsugu Kajita
AD: 飯島広昭　Hiroaki Iijima
DF: 北山創造研究所
KITAYAMA & COMPANY
SB: ゼットン　zetton inc.

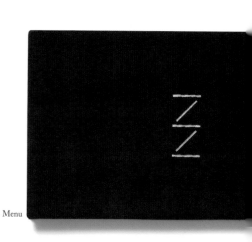

Menu

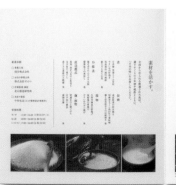

和食レストラン

Japanese Restaurant

阿部
abe

山形・湯野浜にある老舗の温泉旅館「亀
や」が出店した和食店。『正しい日本の食
事』というコンセプトで、海の幸あり、
山の幸ありといわれるほど食べ物がお
いしい山形の料理を食べてもらうこと
で、現代人の乱れがちな食生活のバラ
ンスを見直すきっかけになってくれたら
と考えた。ロゴは、聖徳太子が書いたと
される書物を元に、書家の方にもみても
らいながらバランスを整えて制作した。

A Japanese restaurant opened in the long-
established Kameya hot springs hotel in
Yunohama, Yamagata. The concept was "a
proper Japanese meal," the purpose being
to make people who live in the modern
world reassess their eating habits, by partak-
ing of Yamagata cuisine created from
delicious ingredients obtained from the
sea and the mountains. The logo was based
on a book thought to have been written by
Prince Shotoku, and its balance adjusted
under the watchful eye of a calligrapher.

東京都港区赤坂2-22-11
メイプルアーベント赤坂1F
1F, 2-22-11, Akasaka, Minato-ku, Tokyo,
JAPAN
http://www.kameya-net.com/akasaka-abe

A: 津野恵美子　Emiko Tsuno
AF: 津野建築設計室
Tsuno architectural design room
AD, CD: 水野　学　Manabu Mizuno
D: 久能真理　Mari Kuno
P: 阿部太一　Daichi Ano
DF, SB: グッドデザインカンパニー
good design company

レストラン／バー　Restaurants / Bars

和心料理 寿
KOTOBUKI

元々寿司屋として営業していた店の代替わりに伴うリニューアルのブランディング。寿司屋としてのアイデンティティは残しつつも、創作和食を提供していく。先代からの店名「寿」を活かした形の店作りを考え、「寿」という言葉の字意でもある「長い」というコンセプトでツールを展開。箸袋は地元の大阪湾をモチーフに、また「寿」が地元の網元であったためそのイメージも込めた。

Branding for a renovation upon change of ownership of a business, originally run as a sushi bar, that offers creative Japanese cuisine while retaining the sushi bar identity. The tools were developed upon the concept of the Japanese character for "long," a character of similar meaning to the character that had been the sushi bar's name for generations, Kotobuki (long life), as a means of incorporating Kotobuki into the design of the restaurant. The chopstick wrappers had a motif of the Port of Osaka, and as a local fishing business, an image of Kotobuki was incorporated into the design.

大阪府泉佐野市和泉1-2-3
1-2-3, Izumi, Sano-city, Osaka, JAPAN

A: サイズコア　SIDES CORE
AD, LD: 古川智基　Tomoki Furukawa
DF, SB: サファリ　SAFARI inc.
CL: 寿　KOTOBUKI

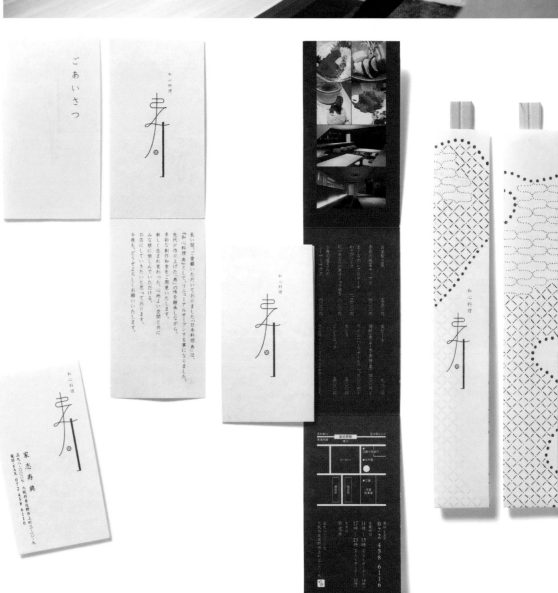

DRINK MENU

和心料理　素月

WINE

RED（フル・ハーフ）
ルイ・ジャド・ボジョレー・ヴィラージュ ──── 三"○○○・二"八○○
（フランス／赤　軽口）
ペヴェロー二・ソーヴァ・クラシコ ──── 二"四○○・一"四○○
（イタリア／赤　ロゼ軽口　ライト系中口）
シャトー・サン・ディエ・パルナック ──── 三"○○○・一"八○○
ドゥクト・ブレール・メドック ──── 三"二○○・一"八○○
ブルゴーニュ・シャルド・ラヴィ・ヴァン ──── 四"一○○・二"○○○

WHITE（フル・ハーフ）
ブラック・タワー ──── 一"六○○・一"一○○

WISKEY（シングル・ダブル）
ザ・サントリー・オールド ──── 一五○・九○○
サントリー・シングルモルト・山崎10年 ──── 四五○・九○○
ブラック・ニッカ・クリア・ブレンド ──── 一五○・五○○
ニッカ・シングルモルト・余市10年 ──── 四五○・九○○
ジョニー・ウォーカー・黒ラベル12年 ──── 三五○・七○○

SPARKLING WINE
ピア・ドール・ムスー ──── 二"○○○
（フランス産スパークリングワイン甘口発泡性）
ビア・ドール・ムスー・ロゼ ──── 二"○○○
ドン・ペリニヨン ──── 一五"○○○

ソフトドリンク
ジンジャーエール ──── 一一○○
コーラ ──── 一一○○
オレンジジュース ──── 一一○○
グレープフルーツ ──── 一一○○
カルピス ──── 一一○○
パイン ──── 一一○○
マンゴー ──── 一一○○
ウーロン茶 ──── 一一○○
コーヒー ──── 一一○○
紅茶 ──── 一一○○

アサヒ・ハート・ドライ
キリン・ラガー・ビア
キリン・ブレミアム・ラガー
サントリー・プレミアム・モルツ
サッポロ・プレミアム・エビス ──── 六五○
Z I M A ──── 五五○
ウイスキー・アンド・ローヤル・ハイボール 0.5 位未満 ──── 三五○

和心料理　素月

125

能阿
noa

「ジャパニーズ ノアの箱船」をキーワードに、日本のモチーフである竹のしなやかで力強さをイメージしている。

An image of strength with the flexibility of bamboo, a Japanese motif, and the keywords "Japanese Noah's Ark."

能阿
noa

神奈川県横浜市青葉区美しが丘
2-20-15 プラザウィスタリア 1F
1F, 2-20-15, Utsukushigaoka, Aoba-ku,
Yokohama-city, Kanagawa, JAPAN
http://dining-noa.com/index.html

AD: 池田享史　Takafumi Ikeda
D: 高尾元樹　Motoki Takao／戸金珠美
Tamami Togane／川内栄子　Eiko Kawauchi
CL: 能阿　noa
SB: design service

和食レストラン

Japanese Restaurant

カスミガセキ
kasumigaseki

和の惣菜や一品料理をはじめ、食堂の
楽しさとバールの気軽さを併せもつ食
堂バール。さまざまなシーンで使い勝手
のよい、温かくリラックスした空間。

A cafeteria / bar that combines the pleasures
of cafeteria-style dining including the range
of side and à la carte dishes with the relaxed
atmosphere of a bar. A warm, relaxed space
adaptable to various occasions.

食堂 BAR カスミガセキ

東京都千代田区霞が関3-2-6
東京倶楽部ビル 霞ダイニング2F
2F, 3-2-6, Kasumigaseki, Chiyoda-ku,
Tokyo, JAPAN
http://www.zetton.co.jp

A: 中川健司　Kenji Nakagawa
AF: 中川デザイン事務所
NAKAGAWA DESIGN OFFICE
CD: 梶田知嗣　Tomotsugu Kajita
D: 加藤小百合　Sayuri Kato
SB: ゼットン　zetton inc.

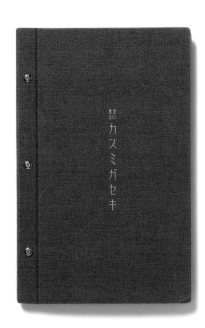

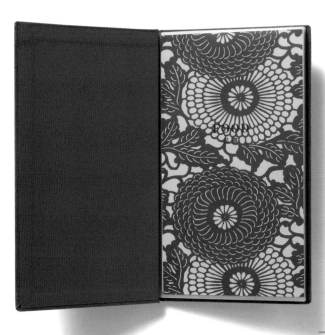

和食レストラン

Japanese Restaurant

元町 ふた川
Motomachi Futagawa

横浜元町では希少となる正統派の日本料理店。フォーマルとカジュアルのバランスに優れたダイニングとして、地元と観光、両方のお客様をターゲットに展開。彩りある盛りつけと美味しい料理が引き立つよう、店内は黒と白木のコントラストを生かしたシンプルなトーンで構成。マテリアルなど細部までスタッフ全員が創り上げた。またツール類もインテリアの一部として機能するよう、シンプルで品のよい高級感を大切にした。

An orthodox Japanese restaurant, an increasing rarity in the Motomachi district of Yokohama. Offering a dining experience that superbly strikes a balance between formal and casual, the restaurant was targeted at the two customer groups of local people and tourists. The restaurant interior is constructed with simple tones that maximize the contrast between black and unvarnished wood so as to highlight the colorful arrangement of food on the plates and the delicious cuisine. The entire staff offered their ideas on materials and details, creating a space that customers would find comfortable to be in. The tools also are simple and dignified so as to function as a part of the interior.

神奈川県横浜市中区元町3-141-8
3-141-8, Motomachi, Naka-ku,
Yokohama-city, Kanagawa, JAPAN
http://www.futa-gawa.jp

AD: 福田 大　Dai Fukuda
D: 横山倫子　Michiko Yokoyama
LD: 長谷麻衣子　Maiko Hase
P: 信澤邦彦　Kunihiko Nobusawa
CL: 元町 ふた川　Motomachi Futagawa
SB: デスク　DESC.

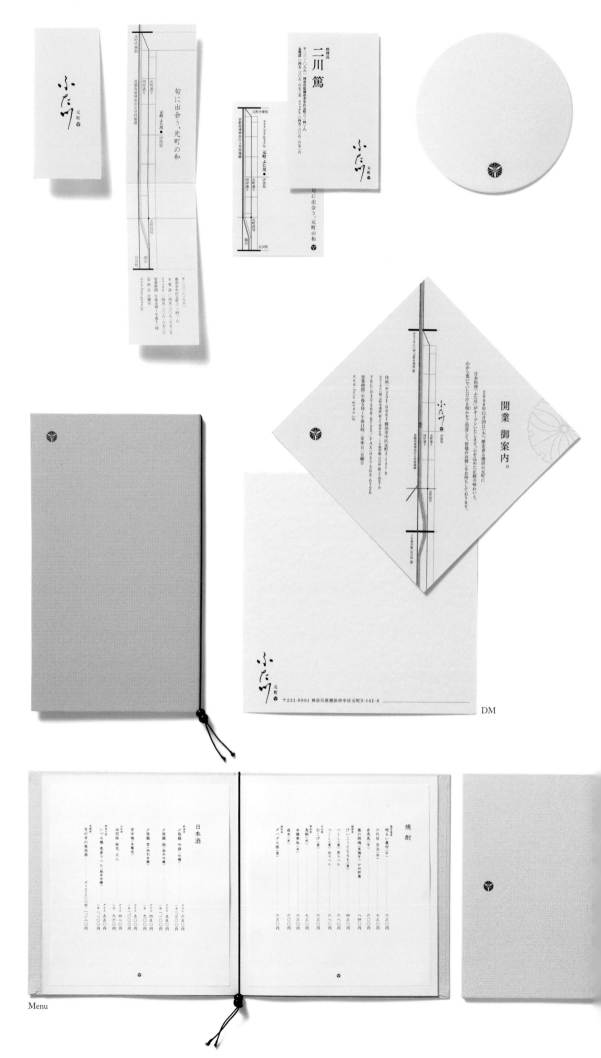

DM

Menu

レストラン／バー　Restaurants / Bars

焼肉専門店

BBQ

焼肉 華火 錦店
Yakiniku Hanabi Nishiki-shop

従来の焼肉屋のイメージとは異なった新しいビジュアルコミュニケーションを探り出した。高級ホテルのような、ラグジュアリーでクオリティの高いグラフィックツールを目指し、クールでスタイリッシュなイメージの焼肉屋を表現している。

A new kind of visual communication was required, something different from the image of a conventional BBQ restaurant. The aim was luxurious, high-end graphic tools such as those of a high-quality hotel to express an image for this BBQ restaurant that was cool and stylish.

愛知県名古屋市中区栄錦2-12-17
2-12-17, Sakae Nishiki, Naka-ku,
Nagoya-city, JAPAN
http://www.yakiniku-hanabi.jp/

A, Space Designer: カフェ　cafe co.
AD, D: 古川智基　Tomoki Furukawa
D: 大久保佳那子　Kanako Okubo
DF, SB: サファリ　SAFARI inc.
CL: キングダム　KINGDOM

GRAND OPEN YAKI-NIKU HANABI

INFORMATION

MENU

EXECUTIVE DINNER YAKI-NIKU HANABI AT NAGOYA NISHIKI

CONCEPT

木花
konohana

日本のすばらしい素材を、大切に丁寧に使用して、ひとつひとつ職人が作り上げる和スイーツを提供する和カフェ。「木花」とは桜の花を表しているため、桜をメインのモチーフにデザインをビジュアル化している。

A Japanese café offering Japanese sweets each lovingly and carefully produced by craftsmen using the finest of Japanese ingredients. Because the name Konohana means the flower of the cherry tree, the design with cherry blossom as the main motif was turned into visuals.

東京都渋谷区西原3-2-4
フロンティア代々木上原1F
1F, 3-2-4, Nishihara, Shibuya-ku, Tokyo, JAPAN
http://www.kono-hana

A: 大坪輝史　Terufumi Otsubo
AD, D: 木住野彰悟　Shogo Kishino
D: 榊 美帆　Miho Sakaki
P: Nacása & Partners Inc.
DF, SB: 6D

レストラン／バー　Restaurants / Bars

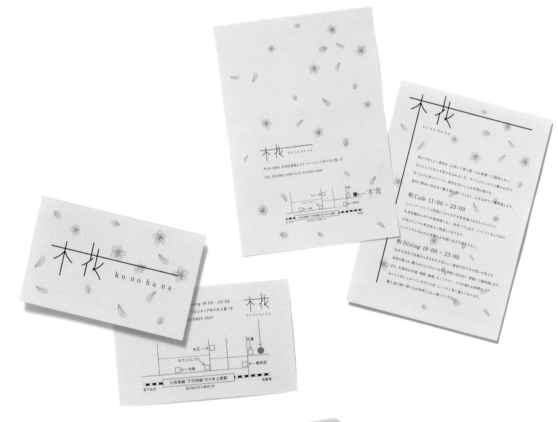

Package for sweets

和 Dining

自然の恵み
〜天然鯛料理・鯛・至高の天然鯛〜

鯛茶漬け
元祖鯛料理の実・発明　　　　　　600 円

鯛しゃぶ鍋
鯛と昆布天紀の出会い渡の香り　1200 円

鯛の活〆造り
落ち着いた旨さと鯛釜蒸菜蒸し　1200 円

鯛あら煮
あたかかく上品な旨味気味造り　　800 円

鯛・約2人前
活天然鯛の荒煮炊き大　1500 円

鯛飯
オーブンでじっくり炊き上げます　900 円

日本三大美味鶏

比内地鶏、薩摩鶏、名古屋コーチンとともに日本三大美味鶏

鳴きさみ茶わさ　　　　　　　　　800 円
男の料理比内鶏卵風《ポトフ》　　900 円
比内地レバー旬野菜炒め焼き　　1200 円
比内もも旬野菜梅肉蒸し　　　　1200 円
比内もも香草岩塩焼き　　　　　1000 円
九条鶏皮旨味串揚げ　　　　　　　800 円
古賀鶏な唐揚子菜　　　　　　　1000 円

大豆を味わう
手づくり豆腐・湯葉料理

木豆腐乳豆腐　　　　　　　　　　900 円
クリームチーズ豆腐キャビア添え　900 円
生湯葉と職方のお吸物　　　　　　800 円
胡麻手出し豆腐国風　　　　　　1000 円
九条豆腐揚げ出し揚げ　　　　　　900 円
昔ながらの餅菓子茶　　　　　　1200 円

味噌料理

旬野菜味噌チーズフォンデュ　　1000 円
島味噌「いか」と九条旬味噌バター鍋 900 円
自家製九条味噌田楽　　　　　　　600 円
ふろふき大根味噌おろし添え　　　600 円
鯖味噌へヒニ「鯖のおかづけ」　　600 円
モッツレラチーズ味噌漬け　　　　800 円

焼肉・韓国料理店

Korean Dining & BBQ

焼肉飯店 京昌園 富士南店
Yakinikuhanten Keishoen
Fuji-minami ten

地元で愛され続けて50年の老舗焼肉店の第4号店。「創業以来変わらぬ伝統の味」というコンセプトを、シンプルなデザインでストレートに表現している。

The fourth in a line of long-established barbecue restaurants that have been popular throughout the regions for 50 years. The concept of a "traditional taste that has never changed since we opened" was expressed in a direct way with a simple design.

レストラン／バー — Restaurants / Bars

静岡県富士市鮫島370-1
370-1, Samejima, Fuji-shi, Shizuoka, JAPAN
http://www.k-shoen.com

A, Space Designer: 小笠原清実
Kiyomi Ogasawara
AD, D: 青木智之　Tomoyuki Aoki
P: 杉山一幹　Kazumoto Sugiyama／
伊藤茂樹　Shigeki Ito
AF, DF, SB: メモラーブル
design MEMORABLE

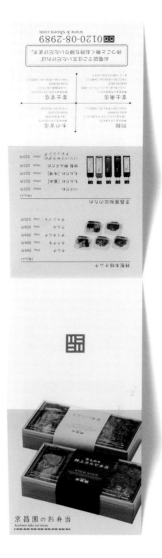

うなぎダイニング

Eel Restaurant

う匠 山家膳兵衛
Usho Yamaya Zenbei

創業大正14年という老舗うなぎ屋。若者をターゲットにした駅ビルという立地で、固定客である高年層をキープしながら若い世代へもアピールするためランチは「老舗店が経営するカジュアルレストラン」、ディナーは「正統派のうなぎ老舗店」という2つの顔を用意した。昼と夜の表情を切り替えるため、内装では照明を、ツール類では紙色や質を変えている。

An eel restaurant of long standing that was established in 1925. So as to appeal to a young crowd while maintaining the older established patrons, the restaurant located in a station building to attract the youth market was given two dimensions: lunch was in a "casual restaurant run by a long-established business," and dinner in a "traditional long-standing eel restaurant." The switch between lunch and dinner was achieved by the interior lighting and the quality and color of the paper used for the tools.

 う匠 山家 膳兵衛

埼玉県さいたま市大宮区錦町630
ルミネ大宮ルミネ2 4F
4F, 630, Nishiki-cho, Omiya-ku,
Saitama-city, Saitama, JAPAN

A, CD: 安藤僚子　Ryoko Ando（MS4D）
AF: 北の工作社　KITANO KOSAKUSHA／
綜合デザイン　Sogo Design
AD, D, LD: 長澤昌彦　Masahiko Nagasawa
LD: 齊藤 純　Jun Saito
D: 中嶋ゆかり　Yukari Nakajima
I: 天本恵子　Keiko Amamoto
DF, SB: マヒコ　Mahiko
CL: う匠山家　Usho Yamaya

レストラン／バー　Restaurants / Bars

う匠 **山家 膳兵衛** ディナータイム 16：00〜22：00（L.O. 21：30）

◯ 鰻重 2,415円 　　　　　　　　　 ◯ 元祖塩焼き鰻重 2,415円

鰻を味わう

天麩羅盛り合わせ 2,310円

マグロのカツレツ 1,050円

玉子焼 630円

鳥わさ う匠山家風 735円

アスパラ2色サラダ 840円

自慢の一品

◯ 鰻まぶし膳 2,100円

◯ 鰻石焼なべ御膳 2,415円

◯ うなとろ丼 2,100円

海老しんじょう 735円

ふろふき大根（ポーライプ味噌）840円

焼鳥（2本）（タレ・塩）630円

うなぎきも焼（1本）525円

刺身三種盛り 1,680円

自慢の銘酒

生ビール（中）‥‥‥‥693円〜
焼酎各種（グラス）‥‥525円〜
　百年の孤独
　中々
　野ウサギの走り
　山猿翠
　森伊蔵
　ハナタレ
　山ねこ
　き六
日本酒各種（150ml）‥693円〜
　十四代
　〆張鶴
　鳳鷹
　八海山
ウイスキー
サワー・果実酒・ワイン
ソフトドリンク

Board Menu

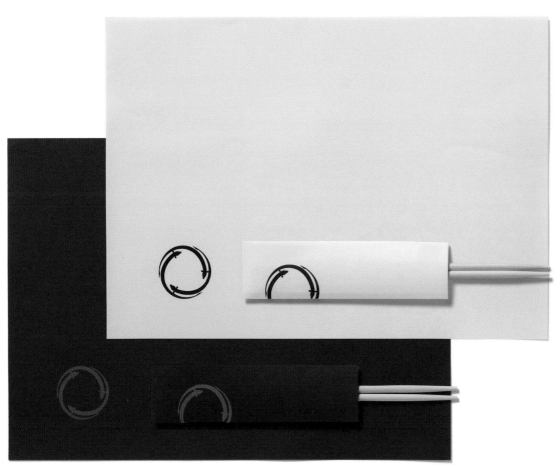

ダイニングGOTOKU
dining GOTOKU

トラディショナルな和ではなく、エレガントな和をテーマに、ロゴ、グラフィック、パターン等を制作した。またツールだけでなく、空間にもグラフィックを展開。VIPルーム3室には掛け軸のイメージでウォールライトを制作。金魚のグラフィックは、水の流れをイメージして作ったロゴマークをかたどったもの。

The logo, graphics and patterns were produced not with a "traditional Japanese" theme but instead "elegant Japanese." The graphics were developed not only for the peripheral tools but also for the space. Wall lights were produced in the image of a hanging scroll for the three VIP rooms. The goldfish graphic was modeled on the logo mark that was based on an image of flowing water.

福岡県福岡市博多区博多駅中央街6-3
博多中央街ビル4F
4F Chuogai, 6-3 Hakataekichuo-gai,
Hakata-ku, Fukuoka-shi, Fukuoka,
JAPAN
http://www.hakata-gotoku.jp

AD, D, LD: 先崎哲進　Takayuki Senzaki
（TETUSIN）
DF, SB: TETUSIN
CL: イートレスト　eatrest

焼肉の Mr. 青木
YAKINIKU NO Mr. AOKI

元プロ野球選手青木勝男氏の手掛ける
店。創業当時から使用しているキャラク
ターをアレンジしつつ、老舗の雰囲気、
高級感をプラスした。
外観のイルミネーションは「桜の花びら」。
「春の夜の宴」がテーマになった。700個
以上のLEDを使用している。

A shop run by former professional
baseball player Katsuo Aoki. The
character that has been used since the
business was established is cleverly
arranged around the store, showing an
appreciation for the history of the shop
and for high quality. The lighting on the
outside of the shop that uses more than
700 LEDs has a cherry blossom and
"party on a spring night" theme.

福岡県飯塚市鶴三緒一本木1117-1
1117-1 Tsurumiyo Ippongi, Iiduka-shi,
Fukuoka, JAPAN
http://www.mr-aoki.com

A, Space Designer: 吉野純夫　Yoshino Sumio
AF: クリア　CLEAR
AD, D, LD: 先崎哲進　Takayuki Senzaki
（TETUSIN）
DF, SB: TETUSIN
P: 大塚紘雅　Hiromasa Otsuka（over haul）

焼肉・韓国料理店

Korean Dining & BBQ

焼肉居酒家 韓の台所
道玄坂店
HAN NO DAIDOKORO

ハングル文字の特徴をとらえ、それを再構築してロゴを制作することで焼き肉の持つ世界観を表現。また、筆文字の雰囲気を使用することで、ほどよい高級感を出している。円形のツールは、渋谷の街でフライヤーとして配布する際のインパクトを考えて焼肉の網と同じサイズで制作し、その後、折り畳んだ状態で封筒に入れてお客さまに発送した。

Expressing a barbecue restaurant's view of the world with a logo that first captures the characteristics of Hangul characters and then reconstructs them. The use of calligraphic-style characters imparts an image of even higher quality. Aiming for impact when handed out on the streets of Shibuya, the circular flyer was scaled to the same dimensions as a hibachi mesh for grilling meat. Designed also to fold up for direct-mailing to customers.

東京都渋谷区神南1-20-5
NAVI Shibuya 6F
6F, 1-20-5, Jinnan, Shibuya-ku, Tokyo,
JAPAN
http://www.foodrim.co.jp/

A: カフェ cafe.co／森井良幸 Yoshiyuki Morii
CD: 金谷 勉 Tsutomu Kanaya
AD, D: 二口 勤 Tsutomu Futakuchi
CL: フードリム FOODRIM
SB: セメントプロデュースデザイン
CEMENT PRODUCE DESIGN

Combination flyer / direct mail advertising

Flyer

American Restaurant

ローリングストーン
カフェ
Rolling Stone CAFE

明るく、渋く、淫らに真面目、アナログ
最後のアメリカ70年代をテーマとした
カフェ&ダイニング。オープニングツー
ルは、昔のアメリカのコンサートチケッ
トをモチーフにウッディなインテリアに
合わせた木の板と厚紙ものの2種類を
制作。各種ツールは基本的に過度な装
飾は避けつつ、アナログ感とスタンダー
ドさを大切に、随所に遊び心をもたせた
デザインとしている。

A bright, cool and loosely serious café
and restaurant with the theme "America
in the '70s," the last years of the analog
age. Two types of tools were produced for
the opening: wooden boards that comple-
mented the wooden interior and the same
thing in cardboard, with a motif of American concert tickets from the past.
Excessive decoration for the tools was
basically avoided, the emphasis being on
analog style and standardization, for a
design that is packed with a sense of fun.

東京都港区六本木5-10-25
ゼルコート 3F
3F, 5-10-25, Roppongi, Minato-ku,
Tokyo, JAPAN
http://www.rs-cafe.jp/index.html
http://sync-g.co.jp

Space Designer: エム&エム　M&M／
磯合恵理子　Eriko Isoai
AD, D: 河上 聡　Satoshi Kawakami
AD, D: 伊東正隆　Masataka Ito
CL, DF, SB: シンクロニシティ　Synchronicity

Discount Card

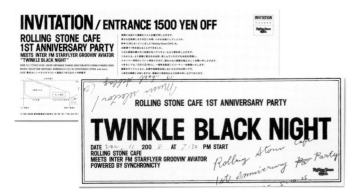
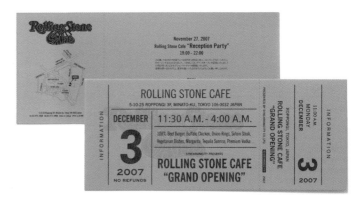

Spanish and South American
Restaurant

ALMA DE
SANTIAGO

リバプールのアルマ・デ・サンチャゴ・レストランは、ペニーレーンの史跡に位置する華やかなバー、ワイン雑貨店、グリル。スペインと南アメリカ料理を目玉にし、元のパブは、教会の家具、宗教的偶像、たわみのあるカーテン、巨大な猿の壁画とともに姿を変えた。メニューのメインは、タパス、グリル料理、ボカリージョ。

Alma de Santiago restaurant in Liverpool is an opulent bar, bodega and grill sited in historic Penny Lane. Offering highlights of Spanish and South American cuisine, the former pub has been transformed with ecclesiastic furniture, religious imagery, swagged curtains and a giant monkey mural. The menu features tapas, grills and bocadillas.

60 Penny Lane, Liverpool, L18 1DG
UNITED KINGDOM
http://www.almadesantiago.com

CD, AD, D, LD, P, DF, SB:
BURNEVERYTHING www.burneverything.co.uk
CL: KOROVA CORP

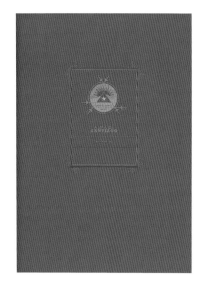

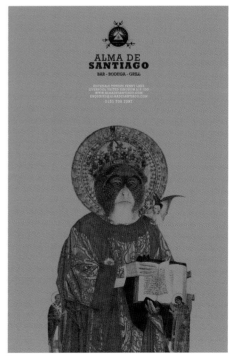

Poster

NEGRESCO DECO

ジャズ・エイジである1920年代様式の
白いテーブルクロスのレストラン。豪華
なグリーン・レザーの長椅子のあるブー
ス、白黒の市松模様の床、おまけにグラ
ンドピアノを付け、緑色、白色、ダーク
ウッドで装飾されている。

A jazz-age 1920s-style white tablecloth
restaurant. Decorated in green, white and
dark wood with rich green leather
banquetted booths, a black and white
checkerboard floor and a grand piano for
good measure.

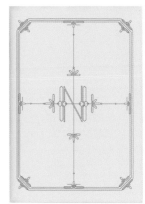

31 Woolton Street, Woolton, Liverpool
L25 8RP, UNITED KINGDOM

CD, AD, D, LD, P, DF, SB:
BURNEVERYTHING www.burneverything.co.uk
CL: KOROVA CORP

Traditional Thai Restaurant

Nahm Restaurant

ナームは、著名なオーストラリア人シェフ、デービッド・トンプソンの評判のレストラン。ヨーロッパで初のミシュランの星を獲得したタイ王国・レストランは、独創性と心を動かされる創造性に価値を見いだす食通にとって、まさに無比の体験。「ナーム」は、タイ語で水の意。ロゴのグラフィックは、このコンセプトを元にしている。ロゴは、メニュー、便箋、宣伝用資料、マッチ箱、また店内サインなど様々な販促印刷物に使われている。水のグラフィックは反転し、料理とワインのメニューを区別する。

Nahm is the acclaimed restaurant from celebrated Australian Chef, David Thompson. The first Michelin-starred Royal Thai restaurant in Europe is quite simply an inimitable experience–for serious gourmands who value originality and inspired creativity. The word "nahm" means water in Thai. The logo graphics were based around this concept. The logo was applied to a variety of printed collateral including menus, stationery, press packs, matchboxes and also internal signage. The water graphic was reversed to differentiate between the food and wine menus.

The Halkin Hotel, Halkin Street,
London, SW1X 7DJ,
UNITED KINGDOM
http://www.halkin.como.bz

AD, LD, SB: Rashna Mody Clark
（Rashna Mody Clark）
Interior Designer:
Edith Leschke（Edith Leschke Interior Design）
P: Martin Morrell
CL: COMO Hotels and Resorts

Cocktail Lounge Restaurant

Mews of Mayfair

ミューズ・オブ・メイフェア（メイフェア
のうまや）は、ロンドンの中でも最も舌
の肥えた住民につくす、高級なレストラ
ン、ラウンジ、カクテル・バー。アイデン
ティティー及びブランド・ツールは、そ
の場所の伝統的英国遺産への敬意とと
もに開発され、また新しい要素の取り入
れは、新鮮さと、洗練された顧客へのア
ピールを保っている。

Mews of Mayfair is an exclusive
restaurant, lounge and cocktail bar serving
London's most discerning residents.
The identity and brand material were
developed honoring the traditional
British heritage of the venue, whilst
introducing new elements that keep it
fresh and appealing to a sophisticated
audience.

10-11 Lancashire Court, Mayfair,
London, W1S 1EY,
UNITED KINGDOM
http://www.mewsofmayfair.com

CL: Mews of Mayfair
LD, DF, SB: Lisa Tse Ltd

レストラン／バー　Restaurants / Bars

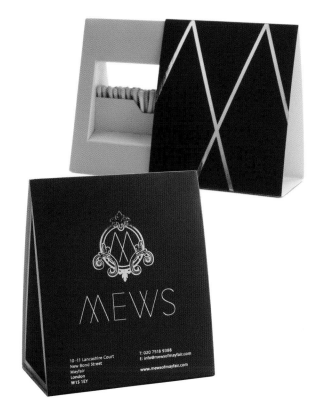

イタリアンレストラン

Italian Restaurant

ボタニカ
Botanica

家具、食器、ステーショナリーなどすべてコンラン＆パートナーズによるデザインで統一されたイタリアンレストラン。「植物」を意味する店名のとおり、落ち着いたグリーンやブラウンを基調とし、葉のモチーフが特徴的にあしらわれている。

An Italian restaurant, all the elements of which including the furniture, tableware, and stationery were brought together through the design by Conran & Partners. In accordance with the restaurant's name meaning "plant," a motif of leaves is featured on a base of subdued greens and browns.

Botanica

東京都港区赤坂9-7-4
東京ミッドタウン ガーデンテラス4F
4F, 9-7-4, Akasaka, Minato-ku, Tokyo,
JAPAN
http://www.danddlondon.jp

A, DF: CONRAN & PARTNERS
CD: Richard Doone
AD, D, LD: Tina Norden
CL, SB: ひらまつ　Hiramatsu Inc.

レストラン／バー　Restaurants / Bars

Cover for Menu

Tokyo Midtown Garden Terrace 4F
9-7-4 Akasaka, Minato-ku, Tokyo 107-0052
T. 03-5413-3282　F. 03-5413-0664
www.conran-restaurants.jp

コットンクラブ
COTTON CLUB

長く使うアイテムは、空間とのバランスを考慮した。インテリアとの相性の良い、赤を基調色に、紙・布・木など、素材の手触りや質感を重視した主張し過ぎないデザインを心がけた。イベント情報を伝える冊子やリーフレットは、ファンの心を掴めるように、期待感や好奇心を駆り立てる編集内容・デザインを心がけている。

The long-use items were designed to strike a balance with the space. Taking care not to be overly assertive and to harmonize well with the interior, the key color of red was coupled with materials such as paper, cloth and wood, emphasizing their qualities and textures. Booklets and leaflets conveying event information strive in editorial contents and design to arouse feelings of expectation and curiosity thereby reaching the hearts of fans.

東京都千代田区丸の内2-7-3
東京ビルTOKIA3F
3F, 2-7-3, Marunouchi, Chiyoda-ku,
Tokyo, JAPAN
http://www.cottonclubjapan.co.jp

A: 森田恭通　Yasumichi Morita
CD: 永井裕明　Hiroaki Nagai
AD, D: 藤井 圭　Kei Fujii
CL: コットンクラブジャパン
COTTON CLUB JAPAN, INC
DF, SB: エヌ・ジー　N.G.INC.

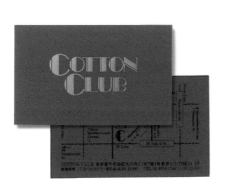

カリフォルニア料理店

California-style Restaurant

ティー・ワイ・ハーバー ブルワリー
T.Y.HARBOR BREWERY

東京では貴重な地ビールを製造する品
川・天王洲のブルワリーレストラン。運
河沿いに位置することから、水色をキー
カラーとし、倉庫を改造した特徴的な
外観をロゴマークとした。水辺の空間な
らではの開放感を感じさせ、またカジュ
アルな中にも高級感が感じられるよう
に、ツール類には統一感を持たせた。

A brewery restaurant in the Tennozu
district of Shinagawa in Tokyo that
produces craft beers. Because of its
location along a canal, light blue was
chosen as the key color, and the distinctive appearance of its remodeled ware-
house was used for the logo mark.
The tools have that feeling of openness
that you would expect to find in a space
located beside water and were given a
sense of unity to impart the idea of "high
quality yet casual."

東京都品川区東品川 2-1-3
2-1-3, Higashi-shinagawa,
Shinagawa-ku, Tokyo, JAPAN
http://www.tyharborbrewing.co.jp/

AD, LD: 西村 武　Takeshi Nishimura
D, DF, SB: コンプレイトデザイン
Completo Design

レストラン／バー　Restaurants / Bars

REAL BEER BREWED
THE TRADITIONAL WAY
FOR NATURAL FLAVOR

LIVING BEER IS BETTER BEER
生きているビール

Specialty brewing yeasts are the heart of quality beer flavor. While these yeasts are killed by pasteurization or filtered out of mass-produced beer to achieve longer shelf life, they are welcome to remain in T.Y. Harbor Beer after the brewing process. Our beers are entirely unfiltered and unpasteurized for maximum flavor, always. Yeast is also a source of various B vitamins and proteins, and is also considered beneficial for the digestive tract. Good beer is fresh and alive, and that's how we feel when we drink it.

ビール酵母にはビタミンB群、ミネラル、必須アミノ酸などのタンパク質や食物繊維などが豊富に含まれ、医薬品としても利用されるほど、ところが微生物である酵母は非常に繊細で、大量生産ビールのほとんどは流通の過程において品質が変わるのを防ぐため、栄養の豊富な酵母を濾過して取り除いています。しかも日本の法律では、かつて酵母保存の生きたった加熱殺菌さえ行わなければ「生」と呼ぶことが許されるため、長期保存可能な生ビールが存在しています。ビール流通を前提にしていない私たちのビールは、酵母をそのまま残した本当の「生」、決して手を加えず、人間の知恵と経験が生んだ発酵食品ならではの恵みを最大限に享受できるわけです。できたての新鮮なものを、そのまま自然に飲む─当たり前のことですが、それがおいしさの理由なのです。

Christmas Dinner
December 23RD 24TH

Christmas Dinner
December 23RD 24TH 25TH

WEEKEND LUNCH

SMALL PLATES

Louisiana style crab cakes with remoulade sauce	1,400
Spicy N.Y chicken wings with blue cheese dip and celery sticks (8ea)	1,600
Shrimp quesadilla with Jack cheese and guacamole	1,400
Mix grilled sausages with creole mustard sauce	1,400
Today's very fresh fish sashimi with special dressing	Market
Jumbo shrimp cocktail with two sauces	1,600
Crunchy fried shrimp with tartar sauce	1,000
T.Y. "Kick Ass" beef and black bean chili with cornbread	1,000

PIZZA & PASTA

Puttanesca pizza with tomato, olives, capers, anchovy and garlic	1,700
Classic Margherita	1,800
Fried artichoke with erengi mushrooms and sun dried tomatoes	1,700
Spaghettini with crab, cabbage and fresh tomato	1,700
Rigatoni with beef ragu and broccoli	1,700

SALADS

Caesar salad (full or half)	full	1,400
	half	1,000
Orange and chicken salad with fresh fennel and smoked ricotta		1,700
Crab salad with avocado and caponata		1,700

SANDWICHES

T.Y.Harbor burger on a homemade brioche bun with fries	(110g)	1,600
(Plus topping ¥100 each smoked bacon, avocado, cheddar cheese)	(220g)	1,900
Grilled swordfish with garlic aioli sauce on ciabatta		1,500
B.L.T.A. with avocado on whole wheat toast		1,400

BIG PLATES

Grilled half chicken "Daisen jidori", senter ale marinated	2,400
Grilled sirloin with gravy sauce and horseradish butter	2,400
B.B.Q. sauce ribs(pork), half a rack with T.Y. original bourbon B.B.Q. sauce, garlic and cheese fries	3,000
Barbequed salmon filet with roasted butternut squash	2,700
Thai style fried rice with jumbo shrimp	2,000

ウォーターライン
WATERLINE

都会の運河に浮かびながらも船らしく
ない外観、「水に浮かぶモダンな部屋」
をコンセプトに作られたバー。洗練され
たラグジュアリーな大人のための空間。
クラシックを感じさせるロゴ、カラーは
ネイビーとベージュを使用し、シンプル
で洗練された印象を高めている。

A bar created upon the concept of a
"modern room floating on water" that
does not resemble a ship although afloat
on an urban canal. A refined, luxurious
space for grown-ups. The logo is classical
and the colors are navy and beige, to
enhance a simple yet sophisticated look.

東京都品川区東品川2-1
2-1, Higashi-shinagawa, Shinagawa-ku,
Tokyo, JAPAN
http://www.tyharborbrewing.co.jp/

AD, LD: 西村 武　Takeshi Nishimura
D, DF, SB: コンプレイトデザイン
Completo Design

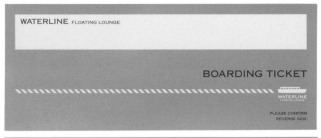

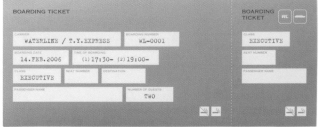

WATERLINE
FLOATING LOUNGE

NIBBLES AND SNACKS

MIXED OLIVES ミックスオリーブ		700
MIXED PICKLES ピクルスとお新香		700
SEASONAL VEGETABLE STICKS WITH ANCHOVY DIP 季節の野菜スティック		700
MANCHEGO WITH MEMBRILLO AND PUMPKINN SEEDS マンチェゴチーズとカリンジャム、パンプキンシード		1000
SELECTION OF FRESH HAM AND CHORIZO ハムの盛り合わせ（ハモンイベリコ、プロシュート、イベリコチョリソー）	HALF FULL	1400 2200
CHEESE PLATE WITH SLICED BAGUETTE チーズプレート	1 CHEESE 2 CHEESE 3 CHEESE	700 1400 2000

APPETIZERS & SMALL PLATES

FRESH MUSSELS STEAMED IN WHITE WINE AND HERBS ムール貝の白ワイン蒸し	1500
NORWEGIAN SMOKED SALMON PLATE スモークサーモンプレート	1500
HON MAGURO TATAKI SALAD WITH CHINESE SAUCE 本鮪のたたきサラダ	1500
WAGYU CARPACCIO WITH WASABI VINAIGRETTE 和牛のカルパッチョ、わさびビネグレット	1800

SUSHI & CURRY

INARI SUSHI WITH MATSUTAKE AND IKURA いなり寿司、松茸とイクラ添え	1500
HON MAGURO SUSHI TEMARI STYLE 本鮪の手毬寿司	1500
TARABA CRAB AND AVOCADO CALIFORNIA ROLL SUSHI タラバ蟹とアボカドのカリフォルニアロール	1500
ASSORTED SUSHI PLATE, 3 KINDS 三種のお寿司盛り合わせ	3000
AMBER ALE BRAISED WAGYU CURRY アンバーエールを使った特製和牛カレー	2300

DESSERT

WATERLINE STYLE ANMITSU (MATCHA AND ADZUKI PARFAIT) ウォーターラインのあんみつ	800
TODAY'S GELATO AND SORBET 本日のジェラートとソルベ	700
FRESH FRUIT PLATE 季節のフレッシュフルーツ	900
CHOCOLATE チョコレート	900

モダンヨーロピアンレストラン

Modern European Restaurant

アイコニック
ICONIC

インテリア、食器やショップカード等の
ステーショナリーまで、すべてコンラン
＆パートナーズによってデザインされ
た、モダンヨーロピアン料理レストラ
ン。ゴールドを基調としたエレガントな
雰囲気と、円形のモチーフが随所に散
りばめられ、優しい印象を与えている。

A Modern European restaurant with
interior, tableware and stationery including the restaurant's business card designed
entirely by Conran & Partners.
The elegant atmosphere based on gold,
and the scatterings of circular motifs have
an understated look.

東京都中央区銀座 2-4-6
銀座 Velvia 館 9F
9F, 2-4-6, Ginza, Chuo-ku, Tokyo,
JAPAN
http://www.danddlondon.jp

A, DF: CONRAN & PARTNERS
CD: Richard Doone
CL, SB: ひらまつ　Hiramatsu Inc.

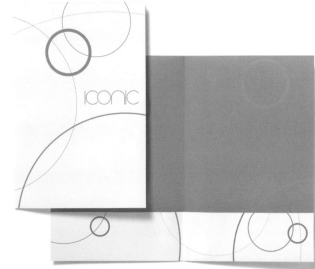

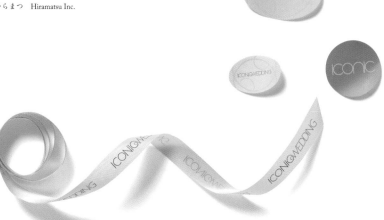

Cover for Menu

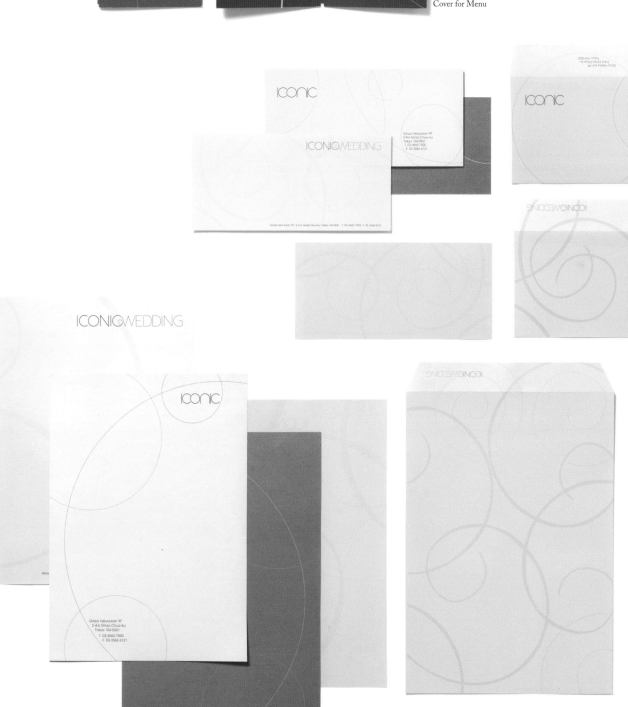

roast

ロンドンの旧市街に位置するブリティッシュテイストのレストラン、roast。イギリスの伝統料理を象徴するかのように、インテリアデザインもナチュラルをテーマにまとめている。

Roast is situated in one of the oldest market in London. The identity and it's applications reflect the natural theme of the interior design as well as the traditional way of cooking.

The Floral Hall, Stoney Street, London
SE1 1TL, UNITED KINGDOM
http://www.roast-restaurant.com

CD, D, LD: Pierre Vermeir
D, LD: Tommy Taylor
DF, SB: HGV
Space Designer: David Gabriel Design Ltd.

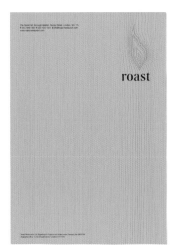

Stationery

Paper Plate Mat

トラットリア・
タナバタ

trattoria tanabata

tanabata は、オーナーの双子の赤ちゃん、
美七海と美夕海の1文字ずつをとって
名付けた、身体にやさしいイタリアンレ
ストラン。2階は家族の暮らす住宅にな
っており、これから始まる家族の幸せな
ストーリーとやさしい味わい、心地よい
アットホームな空間を大切に表現した。

Tanabata is an Italian restaurant, its name
formed by combining one character each
from the names of the owner's twin
daughters, Minami and Miyumi. The
second floor is the family home, and the
happy story of a family that began here,
the gentle flavors and the comfortable
at-home space have all been lovingly
expressed.

trattoria
tanabata

香川県高松市多肥下町1561-3
1561-3, Tahishimomachi, Takamatsu-city,
Kagawa, JAPAN
http://www.77tanabata.com

A: 三好里香　Rika Miyoshi
AF: ドラゴンファクトリー　dragon factory
AD, P: 柳沢高文　Takafumi Yanagisawa
I: 住野真紀子　Makiko Sumino
D: 豊田恭子　Kyoko Toyota
CW, Planner: 川井知子　Tomoko Kawai
DF, SB: ドリームネットワークアクティビティ
Dream Network Activity

Italian Restaurant

トラットリア
ぼーの・うーの
TRATTORIA BUONO UNO

瀬戸大橋の袂・倉敷市児島に位置する本格派イタリアンレストラン。地元の食材はもとより、各地の素晴らしい食材を活かした料理を通じて、お客様との出会やコミュニケーションを大切にしたいという思いのもと、「食する空間」にもこだわり、お客様に食事と食時（間）を楽しんでもらえる、総合的な「食の美」を提供できるレストランを目指した。

An authentic Italian restaurant located in the Kojima area of Kurashiki City near the Seto Ohashi Bridge. By valuing the encounter with customers through the wonderful local ingredients and caring about the "dining space," the objective was a restaurant that offers a comprehensive "dining aesthetic" where customers enjoy not only the food but also the time spent in the restaurant.

岡山県倉敷市児島小川町 3681-13
3681-13, Kojimaogawa-cho,
Kurashiki-city, Okayama, JAPAN
http://www.buono-uno.com/

AD, D: 田中雄一郎　Yuichiro Tanaka
P: 林田 悟　Satoru Hayashida／
田中園子　Sonoko Tanaka（DM）
Space Designer: 虫明昭夫　Akio Mushiake
DF, SB: クオデザインスタイル
QUA DESIGN style
CL: トラットリア ぼーの・うーの
TRATTORIA BUOBO UNO

CMOONE

「カラダを癒す。ココロを癒す。時の流れを忘れるような空間でありたい。」そのようなコンセプトのイタリアンレストラン。表通りから一歩外れたお店では、小さいながらも笑顔が溢れ、人と人のコミュニケーションを大切にした空間が演出されている。

"Heal your body. Heal your mind. In a space where you can forget the passing of time." That is the concept for this Italian restaurant. The restaurant situated away from the main street, is small but full of smiling faces. A place that values communication between people.

大阪府西区京町堀1-15-23 1F
1F, 1-15-23, Kyomachibori, Nishi-ku,
Osaka, JAPAN
http://www.cmoone.com/

A, CL, SB: セメントプロデュースデザイン
CEMENT PRODUCE DESIGN
CD: 金谷 勉　Tsutomu Kanaya
AD, D: 二口 勤　Tsutomu Futakuchi

ESSENZA

親しみやすいイタリアン・レストランの壁一面に沿うのは、伝統的な1950年代イタリアの木製スピードボート「リーバ」を想起させる長い流線型の合板と革張りの長椅子。バックライト付きの木製パネルは、魅惑的なオレンジ色と茶色の木目の縞黒檀、また革はバーントオレンジ色。"essenza"は、イタリア語で本質、流れの意、有機的形状のロゴとメニューの表紙の流れるようなパターンの着想となった。インテリアの基本となっている色調は、反転使用により、料理とデザートのメニューの区別に使われていた。

Lining one wall of this intimate Italian restaurant is a long streamlined wood-veneered and leather upholstered banquette evocative of a classic 1950's wooden Italian "Riva" speedboat. The backlit timber paneling is exotic orange and brown-flamed Macassar ebony and the leather is burnt orange. The word "essenza" means essence/flow in Italian, inspiring the organically shaped logo and the flowing patterns designed for the menu covers. Reverse color schemes, based on the interior, were used to differentiate between food and desert menus.

210 Kensington Park Road, Notting Hill Gate, London W11 1NR, UNITED KINGDOM
http://www.essenza.co.uk

AD, LD, SB: Rashna Mody Clark
A, Interiors: Jonathan Clark Architects

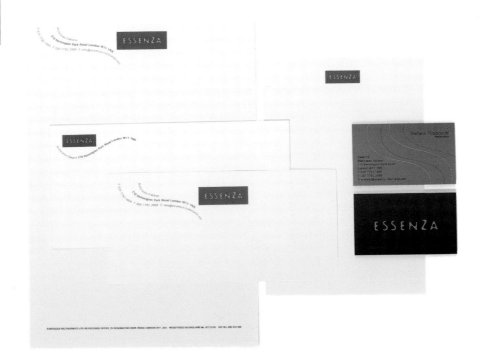

Fusion Restaurant

Nu Restaurant

ミラノでも最も人気のあるフュージョン
レストラン。日本、タイ、ベトナム、中国
などアジア各国のオリエンタルな味と
伝統を現代風に、デザイン的に落とし
込んでいる。

One of the best fusion restaurants in
Milan, where oriental (Japanese, Thai,
Vietnamese and Chinese) tastes and
traditions combine in harmony with the
modern design style.

Via Feltre 70, Milano, ITALY
http://www.nu-pureasiancuisine.it

A: Nisi Magnori／Sabrina Gallini
CD: Mauro Pastore／Masa Magnori／
Alessandro Floridia
D: Cacao Design Creative Staff
DF, SB: Cacao Design

NU 70, Via Feltre 20134 Milano
Cucina Asiatica Tel. 02 26413212 Fax 02 45483930
Cucina Giapponese Tel. 02 89059291 Fax 02 89059292
www.nu-pureasiancuisine.it
Chiuso lunedi

Pesce
euro
*Gamberi in crema di verdura 13,50
*Gamberoni grigliati 13,50
Cartoccio di orata con funghi 12,00
"Kaisen teppan-yaki" frutti di mare alla piastra 11,00
Salmone grigliato 10,50
Branzino grigliato 12,00
Fritto di branzino 12,00
*Piovra fritta 7,50
*Calamaro fritto 8,50
"Ebi-kushi" spiedini di gamberi 10,00

Carne
euro
Fettine di manzo scottate alla mela 13,50
Vitello saltato al miso pesto di soia 10,00
Cotoletta di maiale 11,00
"Tori teppan-yaki" pollo alla piastra 10,00
"Yaki-tori" spiedini di pollo 9,00
Pollo fritto 8,50
Filetto di manzo in salsa di funghi 19,00

Riso
euro
Riso bianco 2,50
Triangoli di riso ripieno 4,00
Riso saltato 4,50
Riso saltato con pesce misto 6,00

Zuppa/Pasta Giapponese
euro
Zuppa di riso 3,00
Brodo di pesce 3,00
*Ravioli di carne e verdure alla griglia 8,00
Udon con tempura spaghettoni bianchi in brodo con tempura 12,00
Tsukimi-udon spaghettoni bianchi in brodo con uovo crudo 9,00
Su-udon spaghettoni bianchi in brodo 8,50
Yaki-udon spaghettoni bianchi
saltati con verdura e pollo/gamberi 11,00 / 12,00
Nabeyaki-udon spaghettoni bianchi in terracotta 13,00
Su-soba spaghetti di grano saraceno in brodo 8,50
Soba con tempura spaghetti di grano
saraceno in brodo con tempura 12,00
Zeru-soba spaghetti freddi di grano saraceno 9,50
Yaki-soba spaghetti di grano saraceno
saltati con verdura e gamberi 11,00
Cha-soba spaghetti freddi di grano saraceno al the verde 10,50
So-men capelli d'angelo su ghiaccio 7,50

Dessert
euro
Daifuku dolce giapponese 6,50
Anmitsu macedonia con gelatina e marmellata di fagioli rossi 6,00
Torta al cioccolato e mandorle 4,50
Semifreddo cioccolato 4,50
Mousse di cioccolato 4,50
Crepe con gelato / mousse 5,00
Gelato misto / the verde / riso / crema / cioccolato 5,50
Frutta mista 6,00
Mango / Ananas 5,00
**Lychees fresco / Occhi drago 5,50
**Cestino croccante con frutta 7,00
**Millefoglie di fragole 6,50

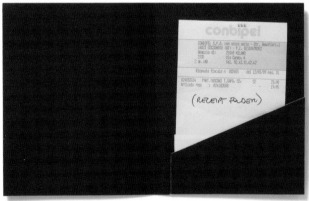

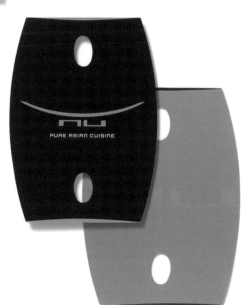

blanco

ブランコは、ソ連時代の都市リーガにあるイタリアンスタイル・レストラン－カフェテリア。グラフィックを支えるアイディアは、スタイリッシュでありながら遊び心を効かせ、空間を地中海の色と光の感覚で満たすこと。「ブランコ」とは白の意、その店名とカラフルなデザインとの相違に、ユーモアのセンスが窺われる。

Blanco is an Italian style restaurant-cafeteria in the former USSR city of Riga. The idea behind the graphic work is to imbue the space with the feeling of Mediterranean colors and light, in a stylish but at the same time playful way. "Blanco" means white, so there is also a humor twist in the contrast between the name and the colorful design.

Galerija Centrs, Old Town, Riga, LATVIA
http://www.stefanotonti.it

CD, D, LD: Stefano Tonti
DF, SB: Stefano Tonti Design
CL: BW Consulting

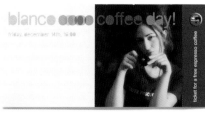

Restaurant / Bar

PARC Restaurant

長い歴史を持つフレンチビストロの世界で、革新的なアイデンティティを創るために、幾つかの分野をうまく統合した。ロゴ・デザインには時代性のある字体を最大限に利用。個々の動物キャラクターと特別なディテールを使い、視覚的独自性を表現した。外のサインおよびサービスエリアは、都会的でありながら森のようなディテールを使い、カジュアルな上品さを反映、また公園が目の前に位置する利点をデザインに取り入れた。

Mucca's fourth experience creating a Stephen Starr Restaurant with master interior designer Shawn Hausman was a study in close integration of diverse disciplines to create a fresh and innovative identity that expressed a unique lineage in the heritage-filled, French Bistro category. The original logo design took full advantage of an original period typeface. The visual identity is illustrated throughout each element of the restaurant's printed communications with individualized animal characters and custom details. With its urban woodland inspired flourishes, the exterior signage and outdoor service area were designed to reflect Parc's casual elegance and exploit its immediate proximity to Rittenhouse Square Park in downtown Philadelphia.

227 South, 18th Street Philadelphia, PA 19103, U.S.A
http://www.parc-restaurant.com

CD, LD: Matteo Bologna
AD, D, P: Roberto De Viq De Cumptich
DF, SB: Mucca Design Corp.
CL: Starr Restaurants

Amaranten

何かしら洗練されたものでありながら
面白いものが創りたかった。それには、
現代に通じるデザインと、レストラン、
バーを表すパターンが重要であった。

We wanted to create something
sophisticated yet playfull. It was also
important that the design be timeless and
the pattern suggest the restaurant and bar
theme.

amaranten

Kungsholmsgatan 31, Stockholm,
SWEDEN
http://www.amaranten.se

A: Peter Ågren
AF: Millimeter Arkitekter
LD: Sissi Edholm & Lisa Ullenius
DF, SB: Edholm Ullenius
CL: Amaranten (Camilla Erneborn)

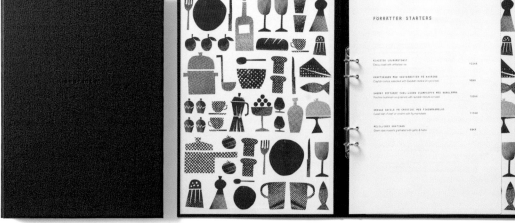

International Restaurant

ESSZIMMER

コンセプトが「自家製の料理（おばあちゃんの味）」のオープンキッチン・レストランのために作られたデザイン。ダイニング・ルームと訳される "esszimmer" や伝統的なスープ・チュリーン（蓋付きの壺）がアイコンとなる。

The concept was to design the appearance of an open-kitchen restaurant with home-style (grandmother's) cooking.
The traditional terrine becomes an icon; "esszimmer" translates as "dining room".

Limburger Street 19, 50672 Koeln,
GERMANY
http://www.abendbrot-im-esszimmer.de

CD, AD, LD, P: Christopher Ledwig
D: Daniel Taubert
DF, SB: F1RSTDESIGN.COM

TOKYO BAR

NYから東京の最先端のポップカルチャーをリアルに体験できる空間というコンセプトを可視化した。デジタル的な感覚とアナログ的な感覚の融合をイメージし、色は東京をわかりやすくイメージできる、日本らしい赤を採用。カラフルな色やビジュアルが溢れる空間の中で印象に残るよう、あえて赤×白の表現にしている。

A concept was visualized of a space for experiencing Tokyo's leading pop culture from New York in a "real" way. The image was a fusion of digital style and analog style, using a Japanese-style red to create a comprehensible image of Tokyo. The daring use of red and white created a lasting impression within a space over-flowing with color and visuals.

277, Church St, New York, NY 10018, U.S.A
http://www.tokyobar-nyc.com

［Shop Tool］
CD, AD, LD: 佐藤可士和　Kashiwa Sato
D: 江藤 源　Gen Eto
DF, SB: サムライ　SAMURAI
［Shop］
Installation: 施井泰平　Taihei Shii／
Team Lab Inc.
I: mashcomix
AF: SOLID AIR
PR: トランジット・ジェネラルオフィス
TRANSIT GENERAL OFFICE INC.

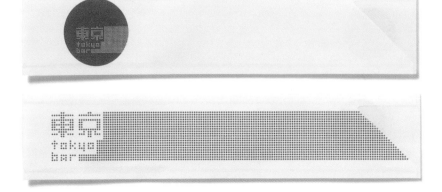

©gion

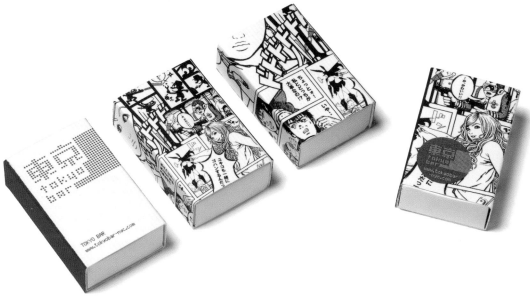

レストラン／バー　Restaurants / Bars

173

マダム・シルキュ
Mme. CIRQUE

フランス各地を転々と移動するサーカ
ス団の女将さん「マダムシルキュ」の名
物料理を、お客様に特別に食べていた
だくお店といったコンセプトで、フラン
スの郷土料理を食べさせてくれる料理
店。クリエイターたちが創り上げた店内
インテリアも魅力的で、肩肘を張らず
に、フレンチを楽しむことができる。

A restaurant that serves French provincial
cuisine, with the concept of an eatery
where patrons are served specialtiés de la
maison of Madame Cirque, the owner of
a circus troupe that moves from place to
place throughout France. The charming
designer-created interior offers a taste of
France without you having to be on your
best behavior.

東京都新宿区新宿 3-29-1
3-29-1, Shinjuku, Shinjuku-ku, Tokyo,
JAPAN

A: e.m.
CD: 青木むすび　Musubi Aoki
AD: 田中竜介　Ryusuke Tanaka
D: 前沢拓馬　Takuma Maezawa
DF, SB: ドラフト　DRAFT Co., Ltd.
CL: ポトマック　POTOMAK Co., ltd

Coasters

Opening DM

未来画廊
mirai garou

昼間は国内外を問わず様々な表現を紹介していくギャラリー、夜はアートに触れながら食事やお酒を愉しむ艶やかなサロンという二面性をもった空間。それぞれの展覧会内容やアーティストの個性に合わせ、素材や印刷方法等にこだわったデザインで展覧会DMを制作。インテリアは、クラシカル＆デコなエッセンスを取り入れながらモダンに仕上げた。

A space with two dimensions: by day a gallery showcasing various creative expression, and by night a charming salon for the enjoyment of food and drink surrounded by art. The direct-mail exhibition announcement was produced with a design that pays particular attention to materials and printing methods and complements the content of the various exhibitions and the personality of the individual artists. The interior has a classical and deco look.

東京都港区六本木5-10-25
ゼルコート2F
2F, 5-10-25, Roppongi, Minato-ku,
Tokyo, JAPAN
http://www.mirai-gallery.com
http://sync-g.co.jp

Space Designer: 磯合恵理子　Eriko Isoai
AD, D: 河上 聡　Satoshi Kawakami
AD, LD, D: 伊東正隆　Masataka Ito
CL, DF, SB: シンクロニシティ　Synchronicity

サロンバー　ヨル
SALON BAR YOL

「CROSS SENSE（クロスセンス）」をコ
ンセプトに様々なセンスが交差し交錯
する大人のためのサロンバー。紙質や
配色をポイントに、高貴さと妖しさ、大
人感などを表現したツール類とした。中
国清時代の木の扉、日本特有の漆、西
陣織、西洋の大理石、レザー、ベルベッ
トなど、日本をはじめ世界のマテリアル
を混在させながら東京的バランス感覚
でミックスした空間。

A salon bar for grown-ups, with various
intersecting styles that accord with the
concept "Cross Sense." With a focus on
paper quality and color scheme, the tools
express nobility, a sense of mystery and
adult sophistication. The wooden doors
from the Chinese Qing Dynasty, the
lacquerware and the Nishijin brocade that
is special to Japan, and the European
marble, leather and velvet create an
eclectic space, combining materials from
Japan and around the world with a
typically Tokyo sense of style.

東京都港区赤坂9-7-2 B-O 201
B-O 201, 9-7-2, Akasaka, Minato-ku,
Tokyo, JAPAN
http://www.y-o-l.jp/
http://sync-g.co.jp

Space Designer: 大月真司　Masashi Otsuki／
磯合恵理子　Eriko Isoai
AD, LD, D: 伊東正隆　Masataka Ito
CL, DF, SB: シンクロニシティ　Synchronicity

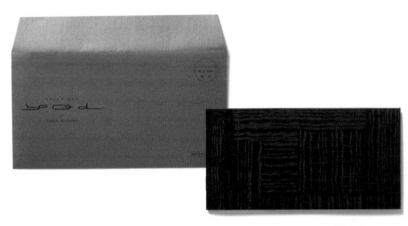

Opening DM

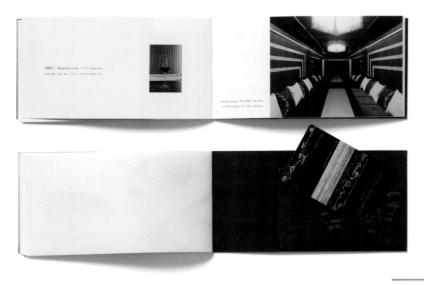

Vegetarian Restaurant

ヌーン トウキョウ ピュアフード＆ ラウンジ

nuun-tokyo Pure Food & Lounge

地球にやさしいピュアな食材を用いて、和食をベースとしながら世界のテイストを混ぜ合わせて調理する創作和食野菜料理店。空間は野菜や果物の色を表現した赤と緑を使用、店内の壁画、ツール、ユニフォーム、ホームページも統一感を持たせている。

A vegetable restaurant featuring creative Japanese cuisine produced by mixing flavors from around the world on a base of Japanese cuisine, and using pure, environmentally-friendly ingredients. The space uses red and green to express the colors of vegetables and fruit, bringing together the murals on the restaurant walls, the tools, the uniforms and the website.

東京都港区東麻布 1-24-6
1-24-6 Higashi-Azabu, Minato-ku, Tokyo, JAPAN
http://www.nuun.jp

A, CD, D, P, Space Designer: 小林俊仁
Toshihito Kobayashi
AD: 中東亮一　Ryoichi Nakatsuka
LD: 日暮武範　Takenori Higurashi
Painter: 望月玲児郎　Reijiro Mochizuki
DF, SB: 温・温 PROJECT
nukunuku-project.Co., Ltd

エヌラウンジ
N LOUNGE

名古屋の頭文字「N」から名付けられた「Nラウンジ」は、焼肉レストランのビルの最上階にあるプライベートラウンジ。「N」のタイポグラフィを大胆に使用したメニューは、折り曲げると三角になり、お客様に手渡す際にインパクトを与える。

N Lounge, the N being the first letter in Nagoya, is a private lounge on the top floor of a barbecue restaurant. The menu, with its bold use of the typography of the letter N, folds into a triangle shape for added impact when handed to diners.

愛知県名古屋市中区錦2-12-17 6F
6F, 2-12-17, Nisiki, Naka-ku,
Nagoya-city, Aichi, JAPAN

A, AF, Space Designer: カフェ　Cafe co.
AD, D, LD: 古川智基　Tomoki Furukawa
D: 荻田 純　Jun Ogita
DF, SB: サファリ　SAFARI inc.
CL: キングダム　KINGDOM

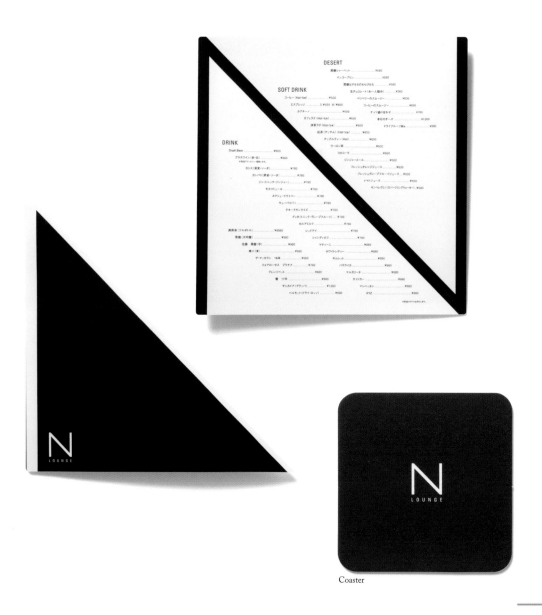

Coaster

ドゥードゥル
Doodle

地下にあるワインセラーを改装したよ
うな不思議なバー。一人でも仲間同士
でもついつい長居してしまう心地よさ
で、いたずら好きな大人が夜な夜な集
う未完成な空間を目指した。

A mysterious bar with what appears to be
a renovated wine cellar in the basement.
The objective was an unfinished space
that, whether you are by yourself or with
friends, is so comfortable you end up
staying longer than intended, and where
grown-ups who like to get up to fun and
games gather by night.

東京都渋谷区（代官山）
Shibuya-ku, Tokyo, JAPAN
http://www.doodle.jp

Interior Designer: 小笠原賢門　Masato Ogasawara
(TRIPSTER inc.)
GraphicDesign: スティーブ中邑　Steve Nakamura
PR: 殿村 博　Hiroshi Tonomura
SB: ダンディーギークス　Dandy Geeks

立ち飲み居酒屋

Standing Style Bar

白と黒を基調に、シルバーでスタイリッ
シュに演出された内装に合わせ、ツー
ルも同様の色使いで設計した。

On a base of white and black, the tools
were designed in the same colors to
complement the stylishly produced
interior. The theme of the design was a
refined sparkle and pulsation and the
printing was done with letterpress.

東京都渋谷区恵比寿4-4-2
クレスト恵比寿1F
4-4-2 Ebisu, Shibuya-ku, Tokyo, JAPAN

DF, SB: ダイナマイト・ブラザーズ・シンジケート
Dynamite Brothers Syndicate

Submitters 作品提供者

New Food Shop Graphics

ニュー フードショップ グラフィックス
２００９年４月５日　初版第１刷発行

Art Director
柴 亜季子　Akiko Shiba

Designer
三木俊一（文京図案室）
Shun-ichi Miki (Bunkyo-Zuan-Shitsu)

Photographer
藤本邦治　Kuniharu Fujimoto

Translator
パメラ三木　Pameia Miki

Coodinator
西岡詠美　Emi Nishioka

Editor
瀧 亮子　Akiko Taki

Publisher
三芳伸吾　Shingo Miyoshi

Jacket Design

Art Director
大島慶一郎　Keiichiro Oshima

Photographer
堀田貞雄　Sadao Hotta

Stylist
優哉　YU-YA（A.K.A.Co.Ltd）

Hair
YUUK（SUPERSONIC）

Make up
EBARA（C-LOVe）

Art
村田朋泰　Tomoyasu Murata
（TOMOYASU MURATA COMPANY.）

Model
Tatiana K.（BRAVO）

衣裳協力
古着王　Furugi-O

発行元
ピエ・ブックス
〒170-0005　東京都豊島区南大塚2-32-4
営業　TEL 03-5395-4811　FAX 03-5395-4812　sales@piebooks.com
編集　TEL 03-5395-4820　FAX 03-5395-4821　editor@piebooks.com
www.piebooks.com

PIE BOOKS
2-32-4 Minami-Otsuka, Toshima-ku, Tokyo 170-0005 JAPAN
Tel: +81-3-5395-4811　Fax: +81-3-5395-4812
sales@piebooks.com　editor@piebooks.com
www.piebooks.com

印刷・製本　大日本印刷

IN-STORE DISPLAY GRAPHICS

店頭コミュニケーショングラフィックス

Page: 216 (Full Color)　¥14,000+Tax

店頭でのプロモーション展開においては、空間デザインだけでなくグラフィックデザインが果たす役割も重要です。本書では、空間のイメージとグラフィックツールのコンセプトが一貫している作品をはじめ、限られたスペースで有効活用できるディスプレーキットや、P.O.P. の役割も果たすショップツールなどを広く紹介します。

A useful display tool for a limited space, display examples which show the harmonization among packaging, shop interior and in-store promotional graphics, a creative point-of-sale tool which stands out among others. This book is a perfect resource for designers and marketing professionals.

995

CHARACTER DESIGN TODAY

キャラクターデザイン・トゥデイ

Page: 232 (Full Color)　¥14,000 + Tax

キャラクターは企業と消費者とを結ぶ有効なコミュニケーションツールといえます。競合商品との差別化をはかるため、企業のサービスを消費者にわかりやすく伝えるためなど、その役割は様々です。本書では、キャラクターのデザインコンセプト、プロフィールとともに広告やツールの展開例を収録。巻頭では、キャラクターが決定するまでの過程やボツ案を特集し、長く愛されるキャラクターをデザインするポイントを探ります。

200 successful characters with each profile, concept as well as the graphic examples. A featured article about the process of creating a character from scratch is also included with useful examples.

984

NEO JAPANESQUE GRAPHICS

ネオ ジャパネスクグラフィックス

Page: 208 (Full Color)　¥14,000 + Tax

近年、さまざまなデザイン作品のなかに、伝統的な和風意匠から脱却し、より現代的に洗練され、アレンジされた新しい和テイストのデザインが数多く見られるようになりました。本書は、広告・装幀・パッケージなどのカテゴリごとに、各分野の優れた "新・和風デザイン" を紹介します。次世代の和風デザインが集結した見ごたえのある1冊として、あらゆるクリエイターにお薦めします。

This collection presents a tremendous array of the next generation Japanese-style design that is currently drawn attention in creative circles as expressed in the form of flyers, catalogs, posters, packaging, CD jackets, calendars, book design, and more.

858

PACKAGE FORM AND DESIGN

ペーパーパッケージデザイン大全集　作例＆展開図（CD-ROM 付）

Page: 240 (Full Color)　¥7,800+Tax

大好評の折り方シリーズ第3弾。製品を守りブランドアイデンティティーのアピールとなるパッケージ。本書ではバラエティーに富んだかたちのペーパーパッケージ約200点を国内外から集め、その作例と展開図を紹介していきます。展開図を掲載したCD-ROM付きでクリエイターやパッケージ制作に関わる人たちの参考資料として永久保存版の1冊です。

This is the third title focusing on paper packaging in "Encyclopedia of Paper Folding Design" series. The 150 high quality works are all created by the industry professionals; the perfect shapes and beautiful designs are practical and yet artistic. The template files in pdf file on CD-ROM.

941

GIRLY GRAPHICS

ガーリー グラフィックス

Page: 200 (Full Color)　¥9,800 + Tax

"ガーリー" とは女の子らしさの見直しや、ポップでありながらもキュートといった、女の子らしさを楽しむポジティブな姿勢を意味します。そんな "ガーリー" な空気感を、ポスター・DM・カタログ・パッケージなどのデザイン領域で、魅力的に表現した作品を紹介します。

A word "girly" represents an expression of reconstructing positive images about being girls. Today, those powerful and contagious "girly" images with great impact successfully grab attentions not only from girls but also from a broad range of audience. This book features about those 300 enchanted and fascinated advertisements such as posters, catalogs, shop cards, business cards, books, CD jackets, greeting cards, letterheads, product packages and more.

1009

NEO JAPANESQUE DESIGN

ネオ ジャパネスク デザイン

Page: 224 (Full Color)　¥14,000+Tax

2006年2月に発刊し好評を得た「ネオ ジャパネスク グラフィックス」。待望の第二弾「ネオ ジャパネスク デザイン」がいよいよ登場。ショップイメージ・ロゴ＆マークのカテゴリが新たに加わり、内容・クオリティともにバージョンアップした "和" デザインの最前線を紹介します。

This is the sister edition to "Neo Japanesque Graphics" published in 2006, and this new book includes even more modern yet Japanese taste designs which will give creative professionals inspirational ideas for their projects. Among various graphic works, this second title features shop design such as restaurants, bars and hotels, also features a variety of Japanese logos.

996

文字を読ませる広告デザイン 2

Page: 192 (Full Color)　¥9,800 + Tax

パッと見た時に文字が目に入ってきて、しかも読みやすいデザインの広告物やパッケージの特集です。優れたデザインや文字組み、コピーによって見る側に文字・文章を読ませることを第一に考えられた広告を厳選します。ポスター、新聞広告、チラシ、車内吊り、雑誌広告、DM、カタログ、パンフレット、本の装丁、パッケージ、看板・サインなど多岐なジャンルにわたり紹介します。

Sales in Japan only.

934

NEW ENCYCLOPEDIA OF PAPER-FOLDING DESIGNS

折り方大全集　カタログ・DM 編（CD-ROM 付）

Page: 240 (160 in Color)　¥7,800+Tax

デザインの表現方法の1つとして使われている『折り』。日頃何気なく目にしているDMやカード、企業のプロモーション用カタログなど身近なデザイン中に表現されている『折り』から、たたむ機能やせり出す、たわめる機能まで、約200点の作品を展開図で示し、『折り』を効果的に生かした実際の作品を掲載しています。

More than 200 examples of direct mail, cards, and other familiar printed materials featuring simple / multiple folds, folding up, and insertion shown as they are effected by folding along with flat diagrams of their prefolded forms. With CD-ROM.

490

DESIGN IDEAS FOR RENEWAL

再生グラフィックス

Page: 240 (Full Color)　￥14,000 + Tax

977

本書では "再生" をキーワードにデザインの力で既存の商業地や施設、ブランドを甦らせた事例を特集します。リニューアル後のグラフィックツールを中心に、デザインコンセプトや再生後の効果についても紹介します。企業や地域の魅力を再活性させるためにデザインが果たした役割を実感できる 1 冊です。

A collection of case studies - with "regeneration" and "renewal" as their keywords - showing commercial districts, facilities and brands brought back to life through the power of design. Focusing on mainly the post-renovation graphic tools, we present the design concepts and their regenerative effects through which readers will see the role that design can play in reigniting the allure of companies and communities.

GRAPHIC SIMPLICITY

シンプル グラフィックス

Page: 248 (Full Color)　￥14,000 + Tax

973

上質でシンプルなデザイン — 見た目がすっきりとして美しいのはもちろんのこと、シンプルなのに個性的な作品、カラフルなのに上品な作品、フォントやロゴがさりげなく効いている作品など、その洗練されたデザインは見る人を魅了してやみません。是非厳選された作品を国内外から集め、落ち着いた大人の雰囲気にまとめ上げた本物志向のグラフィックコレクションです。

Simple, high-quality design work: not just crisply elegant and eye catching, but uncluttered yet distinctive, colorful yet refined, making subtly effective use of fonts and logos; in short, sophisticated design that seduces all who sees it.

1&2 COLOR EDITORIAL DESIGN

１・２色でみせるエディトリアルデザイン

Page: 160 (Full Color)　￥7,800+Tax

956

少ない色数でエディトリアルデザインする際には、写真の表現や本文使用色に制限がある分、レイアウトや使用する紙に工夫や表現力が問われます。本書は1色、2色で魅力的にレイアウトされた作品を、インクや用紙データのスペックと併せて紹介します。

This book presents many of well-selected editorial design examples, featuring unique and outstanding works using one or two colors. All works in this single volume present designers enormous hints for effective and unique techniques with information on specs of inks and papers. Examples include PR pamphlets, magazines, catalogs, company brochures, and books.

PICTGRAM & ICON GRAPHICS 2

ピクトグラム＆アイコングラフィックス 2

Page: 208 (Full Color)　￥13,000 + Tax

935

本書では、視覚化に成功した国内・海外のピクトグラムとアイコンを紹介します。空港・鉄道・病院・デパート・動物園といった施設の案内サインとして使用されているピクトグラムやマップ・フロアガイドをはじめ、雑誌やカタログの中で使用されているアイコンなど、身近なグラフィックまでを業種別に掲載。巻末に、一般的によく使われるピクトグラム（トイレ・エスカレーター・駐車場など）の種類別一覧表を収録。

Second volume of the best-seller title "Pictogram and Icon Graphics". Full-loaded with the latest pictograms around the world. Signage, floor guides and maps in airport, railway, hospital, department store, zoo and many more. Contained a wide variety of icons, including those found in catalogs and magazines, etc.

FASHION BRAND GRAPHICS

ファッション グラフィックス

Page: 160 (Full Color)　￥7,800 + Tax

962

本書は、ファッション、アパレルにおけるグラフィックデザインに力を入れた販促ツールを、厳選して紹介します。通常のショップツールはもちろん、シーズンごと、キャンペーンごとのツールも掲載。激しく移り変わるファッション業界において、お客様を飽きさせない、華やかで魅力的な作品を凝縮した 1 冊です。

The fashion brands that appear in this collection are among the most highly regarded in Japan and herein we introduce some of their commonly used marketing tools including catalogues, shopping cards and shopping bags, together with their seasonal promotional tools and novelties. This publication serves for not only graphic designers, but also people in the fashion industry, marketing professionals.

BEST FLYER 365DAYS NEWSPAPER INSERT EDITION

ベストチラシ 365 デイズ　折込チラシ編

Page: 256 (Full Color)　￥14,000 + Tax

936

　一番身近な広告媒体である新聞の折込チラシ。地域に密着したお得な情報を提供するものから、セレブ＆クールで夢のようなビジュアルのものまで多種多様です。本書では、1 年間（365 日）の各セールスシーズンでまとめたものから、1 枚だけで効果的に商品をPR したチラシまで、優れたデザインの旬な折込チラシ 800 点を収録しています。広告の制作に携わる人びとに必携のデザインサンプル集です。

This book contains many examples of excellently designed, topical flyers, ranging from seasonal advertisements to flyers for a single product. It is an anthology of design samples for creative professionals in the advertising industry.

BEYOND ADVERTISING: COMMUNICATION DESIGN

コミュニケーション デザイン

Page: 224 (Full Color)　￥15,000+Tax

948

限られた予算のなか、ターゲットへ確実に届く、費用対効果の高い広告をどのように実現するか？ 今デザイナーには、広告デザインだけでなく、コミュニケーション方法までもデザインすることが求められています。本書では「消費者との新しいコミュニケーションのカタチ」をテーマに実施されたキャンペーンの事例を幅広く紹介。様々なキャンペーンを通して、コミュニケーションを成功させるヒントを探求します。

Reaching the target market a limited budget: how is cost effective promotion achieved? What are the most effective ways to combine print and digital media? What expression reaches the target market? The answers lie in this book, with "new ways and forms of communicating with the consumer" as its concept.

WORLD CALENDAR DESIGN

ワールドカレンダーデザイン

Page: 224 (Full Color)　￥9,800+Tax

949

本書では国内外のクリエーターから集めたカレンダーを特集します。優れたグラフィックスが楽しめるスタンダードなタイプから、形状のユニークなもの、仕掛けのあるものなど、形状別にカテゴリに分けて紹介します。カレンダー制作のデザインソースとしてはもちろん、ユニークな作品を通じて、様々なグラフィックスに活かせるアイデアが実感できる内容です。

The newest and most distinctive calendars from designers around the world. The collection features a variety of calendar types highly selected from numerous outstanding works ranging from standard wall calendars to unique pieces in form and design, including lift-the flap calendar, 3D calendar, pencil calendar and more.

GRAPHIC TOOLS IN SERVICE BUSINESSES

サービス業の案内グラフィックス

Page: 224 (Full Color) ¥14,000 + Tax

ハードウェアからソフトウェアへの移行にともなう通信関連業、既に定着した働く女性増加における代行業、高齢化社会における介護・医療業務など、社会は今、サービス業の需要が確実に増え、生活に欠かせないものとなっています。本書ではサービス内容を案内するカタログ・リーフレットを中心に、その他広告ツールも併せて紹介します。

The demands for service industries have become an indispensable part of life in the world today. This book looks at the sucessful campaigns of competitive service businesses ranging from telecommunications, internet, finance to restaurants, hotels and clinics. This is a good resource not only for designers but marketing professionals.

930

CORPORATE PROFILE & IMAGE

業種別 企業案内グラフィックス

Page: 256 (Full Color) ¥15,000 + Tax

本書は会社案内を中心に、学生が求める情報と使いやすさを熟慮した入社案内や、その企業の持つ個性を凝縮したコンセプトブック、会社のイメージアップにつながる企業広告などをさまざまな業種にわたり収録。単なる会社のスペック案内だけにとどまらない、企業理念やメッセージを社内外にわかりやすく的確に伝える、デザイン性に優れた作品を紹介します。

A collection of print materials that help create and support corporate image in a wide range of industries: company profiles as well as concept books designed to epitomize company character, corporate ads designed specially to improve company image, recruiting brochures, and more.

877

LOCAL BRAND DESIGN

地域ブランド戦略のデザイン

Pages: 224 (Full Color) ¥14,000 + Tax

地域特性を活かした商品・サービスのブランド化と地域イメージのブランド化を結びつけ、全国レベルのブランド展開を目指す「地域ブランド戦略」の取り組みが全国各地で積極的に行われています。本書ではデザイナーが地域ブランド戦略に関わることで認知度アップに成功した実例を紹介します。地方自治体のキャンペーン展開や目を引く特産品のパッケージ、ショップのグラフィックツールなどのアイテムを多数収録。

This title features the brand marketing strategies for products and services available only in the limited area in Japan. Each brand is created based on the unique identity for the local area, which draws peopleÅfs attention and leads to nationwide the brand recognition.

917

SALES STRATEGY AND DESIGN

販売戦略とデザイン

Page: 224 (Full Color) ¥15,000 + Tax

様々な業種の商品発売（サービス業の商品も含む）に伴う告知プロモーションを商品ごとに紹介。思わず手に取るネーミングや、店頭で目を引くパッケージ、消費者の心をくすぐるノベルティなど、各々のアイテムを巧みに利用した例を多数収録。

Unique and outstanding graphic tools in new product/service launching. Here are packages, novelties and the naming of product offering the newest communication styles to consumers!! With explanation of concept and motive for product / promotional tools.

790

販売戦略と
デザイン
は、切っても切れ
ない関係というの
が、この本のあら
すじです。

Sales Strategy and Design

NEW SHOP IMAGE GRAPHICS 2

ニュー ショップイメージ グラフィックス 2

Page: 224 (Full Color) ¥15,000 + Tax

お店の個性を強く打ち出すためには、販売戦略と明確なコンセプトに基づいた、ショップのイメージ作りが重要です。本書は様々な業種からデザイン性の高いショップアイデンティティ展開を、グラフィックツールと店舗写真、コンセプト文を交え紹介。

Second volume of the best seller titls in overseas. New Shop Image Graphics released in 2002. This book covers the latest, unique and impressive graphics in interiors and exteriors of various shops as well as their supporting materials.

789

SHOP IMAGE GRAPHICS IN LONDON

ショップイメージ グラフィックスイン ロンドン

Pages: 192 (Full Color) ¥9,800 + Tax

コンラン卿に影響を受けたモダンテイストのインテリアショップやデザインホテル、ユースカルチャーの中心的存在である音楽やアパレルショップ、ナチュラル志向のオーガニックレストランやスパ、エステなどロンドンならではの個性的なショップを厳選して紹介します。モダンな最新ショップからクラシカルな老舗店まで、今最もエキサイティングな都市ロンドンのショップアイデンティティ特集です。

Features 97 London shops and shows the intimate connection between the city's history and the street design, which's influenced internationally. The presented examples are dominated by these broad designs: classic, modern, and exotic.

933

ABSOLUTE APPEAL: DIRECT MAIL DESIGN

魅せる掴む DM デザイン

Page: 224 (Full Color) ¥14,000+Tax

ターゲットをつかむために様々な工夫が凝らされたDMを厳選し、その制作意図にまで踏み込んで紹介します。取り上げたDMのポイントとなる部分をレイアウトで大胆に見せていくほか、デザインの狙いを文字情報で提供し、表現に込められた"戦略"を分かりやすくひも解きます。

This book introduces a variety of DM that have succeeded in captivating the target audience and winning their hearts. Many of the photos focus on the quality of the materials in an effort to provide the reader with a sense of what is the most distinguishing feature of DM, something that is normally gained only by picking them up and feeling them.

925

書き文字・装飾文字 グラフィックス

Page: 192 (Full Color) ¥9,800 + Tax

普段使われるフォントではなく、手書きや装飾された個性的な文字を使用したグラフィック作品を紹介。筆文字は力強く和のイメージを、ペン文字はラフでやさしいイメージを感じさせます。文字選びは作品のイメージを左右する重要なポイントです。

Sales in Japan only.

787

FOOD PACKAGE DESIGN

フードパッケージ デザイン

Page: 160 (Full Color) ¥7,800+Tax

896

ところ狭しと並んだ食品の棚で、いかに目を引き美味しそうにみえるか、インパクトと洗練されたデザインが求められるのが食品パッケージ。ショップのイメージと統一された戦略的デザインや、スーパーマーケットのオリジナルパッケージ、形の面白さを追求したパッケージなど、世界中から選りすぐった、新しい発想の食品パッケージを約400点紹介します。

A collection presenting a wide variety of packaging for foods from all corners of the world. The some 400 carefully selected works shown within are distinctive for their unified marketing strategies linked to product and store image, their interesting forms and use of color, their aesthetic pursuits and more.

COSMETICS PACKAGE DESIGN

コスメパッケージ & ボトル デザイン

Page: 160 (Full Color) ¥7,800 + Tax

526

化粧品、ヘルスケア用品（シャンプー・石鹸・入浴剤・整髪剤）のパッケージ、ボトルやチューブのデザインを中心に紹介。また、それらの商品しおり、ディスプレイ写真もあわせて掲載。「今、女性にウケるデザインとは？」がわかる1冊です。

Cosmetics and personal care products and their packaging represent the state of the art in design sensitive to the tastes of contemporary women. This collection presents a wide range of flowery, elegant, charming, and unique packages for makeup, skincare, body, bath, and hair-care products and fragrances selected from all over the world.

FREE PAPER GRAPHICS

フリーペーパー グラフィックス

Pages: 240 (Full Color) ¥14,000 + Tax

907

手軽な情報ツール・新しい広告媒体として注目される今話題のフリーペーパー。専門誌並みに詳しい内容のものから、ファッションやカルチャーなど市販雑誌に負けない充実した内容のものまで多種多様です。本書ではデザイン性の高い、優れたフリーペーパーを厳選し、総合情報・地域情報・専門情報の3つに分類して紹介しています。巻末には各誌の年間"特集タイトル"を掲載。この1冊でフリーペーパーの"今"がわかります。

Free papers are fast becoming the talk of the industry as a new advertising medium and a more casual, inexpensive communications tool. This collection presents a carefully selected array of well-designed free papers grouped in three categories: general, regional, and specialty information.

EARTH-FRIENDLY GRAPHICS

ロハス グラフィックス

Page: 240 (Full Color) ¥14,000+Tax

902

ロハス (LOHAS - life style of Health and Sustainability) とは地球環境保護と健康な生活を最優先し、人類と地球が共存できる持続可能なライフスタイルのこと。ここ数年で日本のロハス人口は増加し、ロハスをコンセプトにした商品の売れ行きは好調です。本書では地球と人にやさしい商品のコンセプトとともに広告・販促ツール・パッケージデザインまでを業種別のコンテンツにわけて分かりやすく紹介します。

"Earth-Friendly Graphics" is a collection of unique graphic communications including package design, promotional tools and advertising for environmental-friendly products and services based on the concept of Lifestyles of Health and Sustainability (LOHAS), the focus of increasing attention in recent years.

GUIDE SIGN GRAPHICS

ガイドサイン グラフィックス

Page: 272 (Full color) ¥14,000 + Tax

875

近年、さまざまな施設で見られる「ガイドサイン」。ユニバーサルを意識した病院の色彩デザインや、地方の私立大学の個性を活かしたインテリアサイン、その他、美術館や空港など、利用者の世代や使用言語が異なる人々が利用する施設にこそ、わかりやすい、優れたサインが見られます。本書は豊富な使用実例を見せながら、時代のニーズに合わせた国内と海外のサインシステムをご紹介します。

Sign systems are designed to meet the demands of the times. It's in facilities used by different ages, or speaking different languages, that the most user-friendly signage can be found. This book presents an extensive collection of photographs, examples of guide signs in practical use, and is an essential reference for designers.

URBAN SIGN DESIGN

最新 看板・サイン大全集（CD-ROM 付）

Page: 256 (Full Color) ¥15,000 + Tax

836

街を彩るさまざまな看板を飲食・製造・販売・サービスなど業種別にまとめて紹介。256ページのボリュームに加え、掲載写真の収録CD-ROMも付いた看板デザイン集の決定版。サイン業界のプロから、あらゆるクリエイターにお薦めしたい1冊です。

From among the many signs that flood city streetscapes, we've selected only the most striking, the most beautiful, the most tasteful, and present them here categorized by industry: restaurant, manufacturing, retail, and service. A whopping 256 pages of signs ranging from world-renowned brands to local restaurants, this single volume is sure to provide a source of ideas with a CD-ROM.

カタログ・新刊のご案内について

総合カタログ、新刊案内をご希望の方は、はさみ込みのアンケートはがきをご返送いただくか、下記ピエ・ブックスへご連絡下さい。

CATALOGS and INFORMATION ON NEW PUBLICATIONS

If you would like to receive a free copy of our general catalog or details of our new publications, please fill out the enclosed postcard and return it to us by mail or fax.

CATALOGUES ET INFORMATIONS SUR LES NOUVELLES PUBLICATIONS

Si vous désirez recevoir un exemplaire gratuit de notre catalogue généralou des détails sur nos nouvelles publication. veuillez compléter la carte réponse incluse et nous la retourner par courrierou par fax.

CATALOGE und INFORMATIONEN ÜBER NEUE TITLE

Wenn Sie unseren Gesamtkatalog oder Detailinformationen über unsere neuen Titel wünschen.fullen Sie bitte die beigefügte Postkarte aus und schicken Sie sie uns per Post oder Fax.

ピエ・ブックス

〒170-0005 東京都豊島区南大塚 2-32-4
TEL: 03-5395-4811 FAX: 03-5395-4812
www.piebooks.com

PIE BOOKS

2-32-4 Minami-Otsuka Toshima-ku Tokyo 170-0005 JAPAN
TEL：+81-3-5395-4811 FAX：+81-3-5395-4812
www.piebooks.com